# ALL THE PAINTINGS OF
# MANTEGNA

## Part I

*VOLUME TWENTY*

*in the*

*Complete Library of World Art*

*The Complete Library of World Art*

# ALL THE PAINTINGS

# OF MANTEGNA

## Part 1

*By* RENATA CIPRIANI

*Translated from the Italian by*
PAUL COLACICCHI

OLDBOURNE

*London*

© 1963 by Rizzoli Editore, Milan
Published in Great Britain by
Oldbourne Press, 121 Fleet Street,
London, E.C.4

*Printed in Great Britain by*
*Jarrold and Sons Ltd, Norwich*

# CONTENTS

# ANDREA MANTEGNA

## *Life and Work*

I T seems fairly certain that Andrea Mantegna was born
in 1431, some two years before Gentile and Giovanni
Bellini who were to become his brothers-in-law. When
he was about ten years old his father Biagio, a carpenter from
Isola di Carturo in the Padua region, consented to his adop-
tion by the painter, Francesco Squarcione. In 1448 when he
was seventeen, this foster relationship had become more a
burden than an advantage to Andrea and he succeeded in
breaking it. He then began making a name for himself both
in Padua and elsewhere.

His extraordinary artistic precocity could still be seen
(before the destruction wrought by the Second World War)
in the frescoes which he painted in the Ovetari Chapel in the
Church of the Eremitani in Padua. The power of expression
and the individuality of conception that these frescoes
revealed were so outstanding that they gave evidence not
only of Mantegna's greatness but also—and most significant-
ly—of the degree of culture and civilization achieved in the
city of Padua in the first half of the fifteenth century.

Biographers have always been puzzled about how
Mantegna perfected his pictorial language at such a young
age, especially if one remembered how mediocre Squarcione's
school was. It was only after the vestiges of Squarcione's
influence on his pupils had faded away that the Paduans,
anxious to claim they had a solid local school, created the

myth of Francesco Squarcione; a remarkable tailor, embroiderer and artistic contractor, whose collections of antiques were said to have been acquired in the course of purely imaginary travels, and whose precious drawings were the work of his worthiest contemporaries. Vasari and Scardeone had strong doubts about him which Kristeller later reiterated. In due course, documents were found proving that Squarcione had been accused of having claimed to teach what he was incapable of teaching, and exploiting for his own advantage the work of his assistants whom he did not even pay adequately.

In 1926, Fiocco attacked this discrediting of the Paduan achievements, which earlier had led to controversy between Kristeller and local scholars. In his first book on Mantegna, Fiocco evaluated the extent and importance of Tuscan contributions to the artistic development of the Veneto during the first half of the fifteenth century. He also stressed that some stylistic peculiarities in the works of Paolo Uccello, Lippi and Andrea del Castagno—to mention only the major characters of this intricate cast—had certainly had a formative influence on young Mantegna. Fiocco's studies are still fundamental for anyone wishing to understand the cultural exchanges at the height of the Renaissance, but at the same time his presentation of other lesser-known artists obscured some essential facts.

These were brought to light by Longhi, in his comment on Fiocco's book. Leaving aside the intrinsic value of Squarcione himself, Longhi drew an incomparable portrait of the man's workshop. Here, apparently, the most intelligent and active men of Veneto and Emilia used to meet. At the time Donatello was creating the equestrian statue of Gattamelata and the bronzes for the high altar of the Church of San Antonio in Padua. These men must have formed a true brotherhood of artists and craftsmen, all compelled by the genius, taste and ability of Donatello. Yet at the same time, their works show that they were all equally incapable of understanding the full extent and meaning of Donatello's study of space, and of his unshakable belief in the value of the individual.

Obviously, therefore, Squarcione's workshop was important as a central meeting-place. Important at least in that it strengthened, by bringing together these different reactions, a coherent interpretation of that part of Renaissance culture that Donatello inspired. No one could deny that at the root of their contribution lies the fact that they went beyond Florentine influence, that they altered, as well as adopted the Tuscan style, and made it useful to more dramatic expression. These artists did this by embodying within the metallic intensity of their colors, a phraseology that was still Gothic and that they would never disclaim.

For the Ferrarese artists who were in Padua at the time, such as Cosmè Tura, the magic of Donatello was certainly exemplified more by the mass of "gold, copper, and ivory" of the San Antonio altarpiece than by the Gattamelata statue. Yet Mantegna was susceptible to the magic of both works, and they combined in his work to evoke an event both historically and narratively. It was typical of his conscious, controlled attitude, which was rarely, however, conceptual or over-intellectual.

Mantegna's evocation of history celebrates not only events but their poetical importance, for it expresses his intuition of a world constituted of imperishable matter, immutable spaces, presences, and emotions. Studying the ancients he therefore came "to love the substance of marble more than the works created from it" (Longhi).

Cold materials lent themselves especially as means for his

expression in providing a firm measure and control over feeling. He produced some almost obsessed transpositions of effects which were fundamentally anti-classic.

Similarly, his conception of perspective was different from, say, the grave and eloquent balance of Piero della Francesca. Mantegna loved stretching the logic of his construction almost to the point of illusionism. He loved to subvert—by stressing his colors harshly—all volumetric values, and to exaggerate his linear definitions. From the possibilities he explored in rendering human dimensions, he found the gestures necessary to re-create an heroic being. In fact, it is because of the brilliant feats of perspective visible in his commanding figures—so greatly admired and discussed by the artists and writers of the Cinquecento—that Mantegna's fame became widespread, while that of Piero della Francesca was confined by his inability to popularize. It is commonly accepted today that the perspective synthesis of color and form, as developed by Della Francesca, culminated in the art of Antonello da Messina and Giovanni Bellini (this was first suggested by Longhi in 1914). A connection between these two artists and Mantegna, historically obvious though it may seem, seems less valid in substance because of the unbridgeable gap between their respective artistic intentions. For Antonello and Bellini, plastic and chromatic values became, in representational terms, increasingly inseparable and as a result they approached all that is ineffable in the human situation. Mantegna, however, saw form and color in terms of point and counterpoint, thus severing an easy relationship of the two in the image itself and, in fact, even establishing a definite order of priority.

Considering his instinctive tendencies, no surroundings could have been more congenial and more likely to stimulate his passion for archaeology, than those of Padua. Even though Renan's appealing but simplistic theory that Padua was the Aristotelian stronghold as opposed to the Neo-Platonism of Florence is now considered by many scholars as inadequate, we still do not have a full-scale study of Paduan culture in Mantegna's time. Presumably, however, Mantegna's learning reflected the characteristics of the city at that time, but the fact remains that neither philosophy nor literature had achieved any appreciable level. Learning and philology were superseded, as intrinsic values, by the new cultural tendencies toward concern with life itself. But the elaboration of a new philosophical structure and even the absorbing of the elegant doctrines and scholarly methods from Tuscany did not occur in Padua though it is true that exiles from Florence found it the only place where they could be understood.

One cannot forget that the surroundings in which Mantegna grew up were those fostered by Gasperino Barsizza, the first teacher of Leon Battista Alberti. Both artists have the same fundamental attitude toward humanity and artistic expression. The representation of man must go beyond his natural dimensions because they wanted to imitate the gravity so admired in the ancients, and to project events and people of the times into the immortal order of history. Both artists exploited the new science of perspective to displace the normal relationship between man and his surroundings, because they were intent on proving that man can master creation and that his work can transcend the individual. This is why the one misunderstood the coherence of Brunelleschi and the other that of Donatello and Piero della Francesca.

The most striking aspect of Mantegna's love for the heroic is that he proceeds consistently from real objects using a spontaneous logic in which good sense guides his knowledge and strictly controls even his most extraordinary experiments in perspective. Even while he introduces in his works those archaeological areas—erudite reconstructions which seem on the surface to be his main characteristics—he is carefully checking their validity from the point of view not only of style, as advised by Alberti, but of history. Certainly the setting against which *St Sebastian* (plates 109–111) undergoes martyrdom is an authentic re-creation of imperial ruins. Mantegna often visited Lake Garda, together with Felice Feliciano, searching for and copying Roman inscriptions. He and his friends would give each other Roman nicknames and assume titles such as *Imperator* or *Consul*, thus evoking visions of grandiose ruins and monuments. The poetic fascination of such settings is to be found in the beauty and solidity of the matter against which the figure takes shape.

Bernard Berenson believed that Mantegna's passion for antiquity was almost an obsession and consequently limited his artistic capacity. Fiocco rightly stressed the romantic quality of Mantegna's archaeological interests and suggested a significant parallel with Shakespeare, even though there is little connection between Shakespeare's tormented characters and Mantegna's immovable, nobly resigned figures. As Argan recently wrote: "Mantegna's art searches for no dramatic effect: it *is* tragedy, in the classic, Aristotelian meaning of that word."

The quest for the equilibrium of the ancients, the nostalgic longing for a more heroic and saner humanity, drove Andrea Mantegna to follow a different road from that of the Ferrarese artists. On the other hand, his correct assessment of the individual's value within the context of history as he saw it saved him from the cultural excesses of his time, such as *The Dream of Polyphilus*. His antidote to erudition and rhetoric was the study of reality. The basis of all his constructions is an analytical and detailed examination of natural forms. The process of abstraction of the planes and outlines which bind those very forms, preventing them from moving and "becoming," operates through exhaustive elaboration. And the image, evolving from such rigorous workmanship, is all the stronger.

Mantegna was no older than seventeen when he painted an altarpiece of great beauty for the Church of Santa Sofia in Padua. This work (it was destroyed in the seventeenth century) made people aware of the young artist. He, for his part, must have realized he had achieved something out of the ordinary for, as Scardeone reports, he signed and dated (1448) it, noting besides his age!

The first records of Mantegna's career are to be found in photographs of the apse of the Ovetari Chapel in the Church of the Eremitani in Padua, unfortunately destroyed in an air raid on March 11, 1944. The original architects gave the decoration of the chapel to two groups of artists: Giovanni d'Alemagna and Antonio Vivarini were to paint the vault and the right wall; Niccolò Pizzolo and Andrea Mantegna the apse and left wall. All the frescoes in the apsidal area were to have been done by Pizzolo, but records of payments in 1449 show that the figures of *SS Peter, Paul, and Christopher* (plates 2 and 3) in the spandrels were painted by Mantegna (several critics had suggested this before the discovery of the records).

Fiocco was the first to suggest that this part of the decoration was derived from Andrea del Castagno's frescoes in the Church of San Zaccaria in Venice, which were executed in 1442 and which Mantegna must have known. Castagno's influence was also visible in the figure of God the Father painted by Pizzolo on the ceiling. The treatment of the drapery both in this figure and in Mantegna's saints is rather trite. But while the figure of God is placed in space with a somewhat hurried lack of precision, Mantegna's three saints, because of their grave presentation and their isolation in a field of blue, rise majestically into the surrounding atmosphere. But the artist's intent was not yet fully achieved, for a single viewpoint was still lacking.

Pizzolo, furthermore, who was sixteen or slightly older at the time, and who had assisted Filippo Lippi in the Chapel of the Town Hall in Padua, performed some extremely clever feats of perspective in his own sections of the frescoes. His studies of the Doctors of the Church are stereometrically graduated and might have been suggested by Paolo Uccello, who was well known in Padua for the figures of Giants he had painted in the Casa Vitaliani, rather than by Donatello. None of Pizzolo's frescoes in the Ovetari Chapel, however, recall his master, Filippo Lippi. But in Mantegna's scenes representing the *Calling of James and John* (plate 4) and *St James Expelling the Demons* (plate 5), there is an insistent echoing of Lippi's themes. Obviously, if Mantegna's taste was ever like Pizzolo's, the similarity was short-lived, and certainly not important enough to consider Pizzolo his teacher.

There is no trace left of Lippi's work in the Town Hall in Padua, but Mantegna's frescoes in the lunette on the left wall of the Ovetari Chapel (plates 4 and 5) are strongly reminiscent of Fra' Filippo's frescoes in their presentation of the human figure in all its physical weight. This was a typical feature of the early Lippi, when he was studying Masaccio and was more concerned with atmosphere rather than with perspective, utilizing landscapes and architecture as prisms to refract the light on the volumes of his figures. Mantegna's use of color in these first two scenes from the life of St James reveals an attempt at harmony that is neither easily discernible in his later works nor adequate to the concept of stone-like figures that he was slowly developing. Expression is achieved here by rather awkward gestures; his figures are pushed into the foreground by the coiling rocky masses and disjointed elements of foreshortened architecture. These elements do not yet jibe with the incredibly illusionistic space.

At the same time Mantegna painted the left soffit of the arch and a gigantic head of a youth (plate 1) at the foot of the next arch leading into the apse. Fiocco believes this grim colossus to be a self-portrait. The fresco had suffered considerable damage even before the Second World War, but it does bear a resemblance to Mantegna's face as we know it from a bronze bust in the funeral chapel of the Church of Sant'Andrea in Mantua. Possibly the young man—he could hardly have been more than twenty—enjoyed making himself look older and giving the face an expression of angry sorrow.

Before working in the Ovetari Chapel, Mantegna must have visited Ferrara in 1449. From existing documents it seems that he painted there the portraits of Lionello d'Este and Folco di Villafora. This proves that the artist's reputation had spread beyond Padua and reached Ferrara, a center of culture. Perhaps his future father-in-law, Jacopo Bellini, had something to do with it. At Ferrara too, Mantegna probably saw the frescoes in the Castello Estense which Piero della Francesca had just completed (now lost), and he may indeed have met the great artist in person.

At this time interest in Flemish painting was at its height —due mostly to the works of Jan van Eyck and to the presence in Ferrara of Roger van der Weyden. Mantegna therefore returned to Padua with a wealth of examples and ideas which became an intrinsic part of his artistic resources.

He exploited it slowly, first with the Bellinis in Padua, then in Mantua. Later experiences, such as his journeys to Tuscany in 1466–67 and to Rome in 1488–89, did not substantially alter his pictorial language. Indeed it became more and more characterized by the reviewing and evaluating of expressive formulas which, though no longer new nor revolutionary, were still capable of transmitting the disciplined humanism of those who had first discovered them, and which still had value in the hands of someone who had something urgent to say. This was true until the end of Mantegna's career when, to please Isabella d'Este, he undertook a series of exhausting projects. Indeed, the main difficulty in establishing the date of some of his works—a difficulty to which most of his critics and students have confessed—depends in no small measure on the recurrence of some of his themes. Subjects and methods with which he had experimented during his youth reappear as much as ten to twenty years later.

The *Adoration of the Shepherds* (plate 44), in the Metropolitan Museum, New York, and particularly the realistic portrayal of the two worshippers on the right, echoes the style of Roger van der Weyden. On the other hand, as Fiocco observed, the chromatic technique suggests that this painting was executed at about the time of the *San Zeno Altarpiece*. The lack of symmetry in the composition, so unusual in Mantegna, is emphasized by the panel having been cut at the left and right, and this in turn emphasizes its Flemish appearance. Some time before, Mantegna must have painted the *Madonna and Child with Cherubim* (plate 31), also in the Metropolitan Museum, which reveals clear connections with Jacopo Bellini. However, the child's foot pushing against the parapet has the effect of drawing the picture out of the foreground, thus giving it a monumental character that was most uncommon at the phase of Mantegna's development. There is nothing of Lippi's tender playfulness in the Child's face, yet traces of Fra' Filippo continued to linger in Mantegna's work.

This is particularly true of the beautiful *Madonna and Child* (plate 126) in the Poldi Pezzoli Museum, Milan, which, if examined within the context of Mantegna's work recently exhibited, must be a painting of his full maturity—even though it does precede another splendid treatment of the same theme in the Accademia Carrara, Bergamo (plate 138), a picture permeated with the feeling of intense depression that marks the artist's last works. Typical of this last period are the *Savior* of 1493 at Correggio (plate 127) and the foreshortened *Dead Christ* (plate 130) in the Brera, Milan. Both these paintings, moreover, cling to Donatello's original influence. This is even more marked in the *Christ Child Standing in a Niche* in Washington (plate 30). In my view the latter should be dated at the same time as the last *Stories of St James* in Padua, that is to say about 1455, or else at about the same time as the *Madonna with Sleeping Child* in the Staatliches Museen, Berlin (plate 69), which was probably painted during the early part of Mantegna's stay in Mantua.

A further examination of the frescoes in the Ovetari Chapel at Padua—which the artist resumed after his brief visit to Ferrara—leads one to think that there is no problem about the order in which Mantegna executed first the remaining four scenes from the *Life of St James* (plates 6–11, 22–29), and then the last two from the life of *St Christopher* (plates 36–43). The traditional version (confirmed by Fiocco) is consistent and rational: the execution followed the course of the story and culminated, following Pizzolo's death, in the *Martyrdom of St James* (plate 23), after which Mantegna went on to fresco the opposite wall. But Eisler, Ragghianti and

E. Tietze-Conrat have objected, on stylistic grounds, to placing the *Martyrdom of St Christopher* at the end of the series. Erice Rigoni, after a close study of relevant documents and noting that in 1451 Mantegna received several payments, both alone and in conjunction with Assuino, suggested that he was then working on the scenes of St Christopher rather than on those of St James. It seems technically improbable, however, since the whole right wall was covered by scaffolding, that Mantegna would agree to work on the bottom row with hardly any light. I believe, moreover, that the suggestion that the perspective is less ambitious and successful on the St Christopher wall can equally imply that it was not successful because it was too ambitious: that is to say, instead of painting for a viewer standing well beneath his picture, Mantegna concentrated the whole compartment from a single, imaginary point of view outside the chapel, and generally coordinated his perspective effect round the Ionic column separating the scene the *Martyrdom of St Christopher* from that of his *Removal*. The composite character of the fresco forecasts the scheme of the *San Zeno Altarpiece*. The fact that Ansuino received his payments in the early part of 1451 leads one to think that Mantegna had already made good progress with his own frescoes on the left wall. If this was rejected, one would be forced to conclude that Ansuino and Bono da Ferrara were the actual— and very awkward—antecedents of Mantegna's figures. I believe that after Pizzolo died, that is, after December 18, 1453, Mantegna executed the *Martyrdom of St James* (plates 23 and 28–29) and, almost simultaneously, the *Assumption* in the apse (plates 33–35). This theory is supported by a similar composition for the *St Euphemia* (plate 32) in Naples, painted in 1454, above all now that its landscape has been restored.

Though Mantegna's development was based on an un-changing concept of austere concision, it is none the less complex. The lunette with *SS Anthony and Bernardino Holding the Monogram of Christ in a Wreath* (plate 12) is perfectly consistent in style with the scenes from the *Life of St James*. The lunette was originally placed above the main entrance of the Church of San Antonio in Padua, and it is dated 1452. On the other hand, the scheme of the *St Luke Polyptych* (plates 13–21), now in the Brera Gallery, seems over-formal, though undoubtedly its original great frame, so admired by those who described it, helped to set off the powerful figures against the gold background. Against this luminous surrounding, the brown and pink robes of the saints in their niches create a wonderful balance of color which culminates in the triptych of the *Pietà*, at the top center (plates 14–15, 17). Mantegna had thought about the use of those dark and pink tonalities when he lived with the Bellini family, but he had found a way of applying them so as to suggest a precious quality in simple material, and creating some astonishing mineral mixtures on which features, drapery, and fruit would remain impressed for ever. These, indeed, are the same elements that form the opal, quartz, onyx, and agate hues of the Berlin *Presentation in the Temple* (plate 66). Within the stupendous marble frame the gestures of the figures seem more eternal than time: Joseph stares from the center and the two figures at the sides turn their gaze away toward some distant point, thereby showing that their presence in this touching geometrical group is merely a formality.

In panels such as the *Presentation*, and the *Assumption* in the Ovetari Chapel, probably executed between 1454 and 1457, one can see Mantegna trying to refine the narration to the point where his language is expressed purely by the movement of volumes which are stressed or softened by the use of color. These are studies in counterpoint, and they are no less poetic—at this phase—than Giovanni Bellini's paintings in which plastic and chromatic values are inseparable.

The same analysis of the elements of Mantegna's composition applies to the scenes in the Ovetari Chapel, where the narration is freer. This, I feel, is the saving grace which makes these frescoes something more than a mosaic of archaeological fragments (especially criticized by Berenson). In the scenes from the *Life of St James* the blending of Roman architecture with figures and foreshortened glimpses of everyday fifteenth-century life achieves the happy coexistence that had been Alberti's ideal. In *St James Baptizing Hermogenes* (plate 6) the two children in the foreground and the shop seen through the arches at the bottom do not clash at all with the solemn ceremony portrayed in the center. This is because they are smoothly immersed in the light effect that Mantegna had learned from Piero della Francesca (though he would never achieve the vitality that Piero gave to his scenes by blending light with color). Here clear outlines establish each form and transfix them. Note the gesture of the soldier in *St James Healing the Cripple* (plate 22) as he pushes back the standard-bearer (plate 27), and James pauses on his way to martyrdom (plate 24). How necessary that fleeting moment is for the balance of the whole scene! Yet every suggestion of movement is absorbed by the economy of the figure itself and in this way the static vision of the ensemble is kept intact. In the middle distance we see the famous "standing warrior" resting his shield on the ground, so strongly reminiscent of Donatello's *St George*. But by turning the man's head to a three-quarter profile, Mantegna has completed the sinusoidal movement which

Donatello, by leaving it unfinished, had made so potentially impressive. Consequently Mantegna's figure appears unnaturally static (plate 22).

Since earliest studies it has been held that the figures in the scenes from the *Life of St Christopher* (plates 36–43) were not imitations of ancient statues but portraits of live models. Vasari claims that this was because Squarcione found much to criticize in his pupil's decorations in the Ovetari Chapel. Vasari's explanation appears improbable because, in the first place, when the frescoes were being executed, Mantegna had severed his legal connection with Squarcione (after a long and bitter judicial controversy, which must have greatly strained their relationship). In the second place, Squarcione, though admittedly a better critic than an artist, was certainly not the most likely person to whom Mantegna might have turned for advice.

Mantegna was to complete a wall, and he must to some extent have been familiar with its general decorative scheme. Even the first scenes of the upper row, painted by Ansuino probably assisted by Giovanni da Camerino, reveal a parallel with Mantegna's frescoes on the opposite wall that cannot be due to coincidence.

That Mantegna inspired the others is an acceptable theory. In *St Christopher Carrying the Christ Child* Bona da Ferrara shows some grasp of Mantegna's theories, but if one compares the landscape of this fresco with that of the *Martyrdom of St James* (plate 29) one sees immediately how Bono merely inserted into his composition a number of elements copied from life and fragments of ancient ruins with no consideration for distances and distribution of light. He had studied the Mantegna carefully, but had failed to understand him in full. The same is generally true, perhaps more so, of *St Christopher Addressing the Crowd*. Here the perspective is completely crippled although some of the gigantic figures and architectural elements are clearly after Mantegna.

Aware that his own complex experiences were being misunderstood, Mantegna was obviously anxious to establish some form of demarcation between his own work and that of his collaborators. This is probably why he united in a single sequence the two scenes of the *Martyrdom of St Christopher* (plates 36–37). These are planned from a point of view just outside the columned chapel at the right. The symmetry of the central building, however, is brought forward, so that the column separating the two scenes becomes its axis; and the slanted background at the right is developed through the three arches, continuing the movement of the saint's huge body as the soldiers carry it away. Much has been made of the fact that this fresco was painted without consideration of the spectator's own eye-level. This could well be explained by Mantegna's desire to emphasize the enormous mass of Christopher's dead body, a monstrous rather than tragic vision. The apathy of Mantegna's figures becomes, in this case, a lack of participation by the artist in the theme he is developing. He is in fact relating a story, a legend, rather, and it would seem that he was more amused than moved by the invention of his colossal Christopher. He was probably well trained to observe the exaggerations of nature but found it difficult to translate them into the stony world of his figures. He expresses here his own surprise—with no grotesque deformation—merely by portraying the astonishment of the spectators among the fantastic, almost absurd succession of buildings.

He was probably still working in the Ovetari Chapel when he received the commission for the three-part *San Zeno Altarpiece* at Verona. He planned this as a forcing of all the perspective knowledge of his time within a frontal scheme.

This and other paintings of this period show that the artist was then attempting to achieve either a misleadingly realistic form of perspective, or one developed to the point of distortion, to which, however, he wished to give some metaphysical power. He was obsessed by the problem of how to create, within the dynamics of his newly discovered pictorial space, images that would command respect and even, indeed, worship. The head of St Lawrence in the right panel of the *San Zeno Altarpiece* is very similar to that of the small *St George*, in the Venice Accademia (plate 60), and the landscape of the latter strongly recalls that of the *Martyrdom of St James*. The principle of the frontal image can also be seen in the *Martyrdom of St Sebastian*, in Vienna (plate 61). Here, however, the planes are more complex and are most effectively lit. The pillar of the round arch, the broken bas-relief in the middle distance, the enormous heads and other fragments result in a varying contrast of tones and solidity with the cold body of the saint in the foreground. The scheme that Mantegna established here became fundamental to the North Italian painters. It was repeated almost exactly by Foppa in a similar composition in the Castello Sforzesco in Milan.

In the *Agony in the Garden* (plates 45–47) in the National Gallery, London, the somber silhouette of Christ kneeling in prayer is the central figure against the background: a distant city at the foot of a Dolomitic range of mountains. Withered trees and apocalyptic birds in the foreground seem to watch over the sleeping Apostles as Judas advances from the right with armed soldiers. The extraordinary dimensional relationships in this composition—which otherwise reveals Piero della Francesca's influence—do not in the least spoil the beauty of the landscape. Everything seems alive in this rarefied atmosphere: from the five little angels in the sky bearing the instruments of the Passion, to the rabbits playing everywhere and symbolizing, through their fertility, the hope of Redemption.

The same elements of rocks and lighting in a hard, though strangely roseate world can be seen in the *St Jerome in the Wilderness* (plate 65) in São Paulo, Brazil. This is yet another case in which Mantegna showed that he could freely do without archaeology when illustrating a story which is older than history itself.

In the *Adoration of the Shepherds* in New York (plate 44) Mantegna was still seeking for a complex symmetry, such as he had found in the *Agony in the Garden* (plate 45). But whereas in the *Agony* the motif of Judas leading the soldiers is successful, in the *Adoration* the angels calling the shepherds, the poor arriving with their humble gifts and the quiet river are all overpowered by the artist's insistence on the ugliness of the two peasants in their over-pious (and extremely uncomfortable) kneeling position.

It is not easy to establish exactly which is the panel that Mantegna painted for the Podestà of Padua, Giacomo Antonio Marcello, and which thus postponed his move to Mantua where Marquis Gonzaga was waiting for him. One of the reasons which led the artist to accept the appointment of Court Painter to the Mantuan rulers (a much envied position, although not exempt from irritating demands) was his hope of escaping the epidemic of plague which ravaged Padua between 1456 and 1457. If this is the case, then it is quite likely that as E. Tietze-Conrat suggested, the panel he painted for Marcello was a *St Sebastian*, the protector from plagues, perhaps the one now in Vienna. Once the epidemic was over, the artist seemed less eager to leave Padua, notwithstanding the promises and pressures of the Gonzagas, who decided to appoint Mantegna rather than Michele Pannonio.

Ludovico Gonzaga was probably influenced in this choice by the Papal protonotary Gregorio Correr, a scholarly humanist and friend of Cecilia Gonzaga, who had earlier commissioned the *San Zeno Altarpiece*.

In this work (plates 48–59) Mantegna's love of classical antiquity is expressed in his sumptuous and exuberant treatment of the architecture, a treatment which was to become a text for the Northern Italians. The magic of Donatello's altar in the Santo is transformed here into a kind of worship of the splendidly cold, jewel-like elements of the decorations (plates 54–55). Similarly, the power of each figure lies in its plastic elements. But, ultimately, the absolute representational importance of the composition is to be found in the astonishing perfection with which each volume is calibrated within the general perspective. One cannot, for instance, visualize the tripartite composition without its frame. And it was indeed deplorable that after Napoleon's depredations, Verona was only given back the larger panels. The magnificent predella was divided between the Louvre (plate 57) and the Museum in Tours (plates 56 and 58).

Mantegna had now perfected his condensation of volumes, which was related to an equally great dissonance of colors. The *Madonna with Sleeping Child* in Berlin (plate 69) typifies the artist's silent eloquence which again could have been stimulated in him only by Piero della Francesca. The elliptical movement of the figure of the Virgin in Donatello's high altar is replaced in the *San Zeno Altarpiece* by the two wheels at the top and bottom of her throne: two circular movements brought to a standstill, like the soundless choir of the chubby angels framing the Mother and Child (plate 52). In this perspective "box" there are no exaggerations or incidental features. Beneath it were the three scenes of the predella: the *Agony in the Garden* (plate 56), the *Crucifixion* (plate 57) and

the *Resurrection* (plate 58). The consistency of their arrangement (plate 48) is perfect: in the center stand the three
crosses on a great stone platform, surrounded by the sorrow-
ing Marys and indifferent soldiers; at the sides, the rocky
niche in which Christ rises before the incredulous, terrified
sentries is balanced on the left by the golden twilight glow-
ing through the trees, as Christ prays to His Father. In the
panels above, the figures' faces are apathetic; in the predella,
human grief is studied to an almost anatomical degree. The
result is an image which is as irrevocable as the study itself
is merciless. These paintings are truly spellbinding.

From 1459 onwards Mantegna was in Mantua, working
for the Gonzaga family whose palace chapel had been
decorated earlier under his supervision. The decorations
apparently included a triptych of small dimensions but
majestically effective. This might or might not be the one
now in Florence (plates 70–74); there are doubts, especially
about two sections (plates 71–73). Mantegna's works in this
phase are difficult to place chronologically on the basis of
stylistic evidence alone. He seems to have been torn between
the study of the majestic effects achieved through miniatures
and that of decorative details in his larger pictures. The only
dates that can be established with reasonable certainty in this
period are that of the *Portrait of Cardinal Lodovico Mezzarota*
in Berlin (plate 67), possibly executed during the Council of
Ferrara between 1459 and 1460, and the small *Portrait of
Cardinal Francesco Gonzaga* in Naples (plate 68), probably
painted shortly after. Certainly during 1463 Mantegna was
providing drawings for the frescoes in Cavriana Castle, later
executed by Samuele da Tardate and considered one of the
richest and oldest examples of decoration in the classic style.
We also know that he was working on some panels for the
Mantua Chapel, on drawings for tapestries and on copying

portraits—for, oddly enough, although he greatly respected him as an artist, Lodovico Gonzaga often employed Mantegna as a mere craftsman.

In 1466 Mantegna apparently went to Florence and discussed with Leon Battista Alberti the tribune of the Annunziata which Gonzaga had promised to build and Alberti to design. Obviously Mantegna's aesthetic views were thought important, for the following year his advice was again sought in connection with the decoration of the Cemetery in Pisa where, in the background of Gozzoli's fresco of the *Tower of Babel*, some critics find evidence of Mantegna's influence.

The small *Florence Triptych* in the Uffizi (plates 70–74) seems to have been executed at about the same time as the predella of the *San Zeno Altarpiece*. This is particularly true of the luminous atmosphere in the two open-air scenes, the *Adoration of the Magi* (plates 72–73) and the *Ascension* (plate 71). Another painting, *The Death of the Virgin* (plate 76) recalls the main panel of the *San Zeno Altarpiece* because of the grandeur of its scenic structure, though the *Death of the Virgin* is actually rather small in dimension. (See Longhi's reconstruction in the comment on plate 76.) The third part of the *Florence Triptych*, the *Circumcision* (plate 70), suggests Mantegna was experimenting here with the grand effects that he was to achieve in the famous *Camera degli Sposi* in Mantua (plates 80–107). Though rather precious, the *Florence Triptych* is very effective; the fascinating tale of the Magi, represented a few decades earlier by the Gothic painters, is all here, but Mantegna replaced their somewhat hot-house atmosphere with the crystal-clear mountain air of the Alps.

Only one other work is perhaps as finely executed as the *Florence Triptych* at this stage, besides the *Death of the Virgin:*

that is the *Judith* in Washington (plate 108). The two women standing under the white triangle of the tent form an admirable group balanced round the half-hidden tent-pole behind them. Their shapely forms and impassive expressions conceal a violence revealed only by a few acid contrasts of color. It is difficult, once again, to date this work, though it must surely be close to the *Madonna of the Stonecutters* in Florence (plates 122–125). This small painting fits a description by Vasari, who claims that Mantegna painted it in Rome. This would place it in 1488, when the artist was decorating the Chapel of Innocent VIII and experimenting in his spare time with large-scale miniatures.

The lack of certainty about the dates of the *Florence Triptych* and allied works partly disappears when we come to examine the *Portrait of Cardinal Carlo de' Medici* (plate 78), and the *Portrait of a Gentleman*—perhaps Pannonius—in Washington (plate 79). Both these paintings are not far removed from the frescoes in the *Camera degli Sposi*, possibly begun in 1468 and finished in 1474. In the same period must belong the great *St Sebastian* in the Louvre (plates 109–111) which arrived in France in 1481 and became one of the favorite examples for Northern artists looking for a sumptuous classical style. Here, solid matter is minutely outlined in ruthless light, and the artist's imagination has run wild in a landscape similar to that in the *Camera degli Sposi* (plates 92 and 98). It is as if Mantegna, having inspired the Ferrarese, was now himself fired by their ambition to create an even more disorganized and fascinating universe.

In the *Camera degli Sposi* (plates 80–107) flights of fancy, decorative preciousness, and minute study are all subservient to a complex overriding concept. This was a norm that was to remain fundamental for innovators such as Bramante and his Lombard followers, for Melozzo, Correggio, the Ferrarese artists of the early Cinquecento and the Venetians, especially Paolo Veronese. Even some motifs on the vaulting of the Sistine Chapel seem inspired by the Mantuan ceiling: details of cherubs, for instance, which Michelangelo could well have lifted from a study of Mantegna's drawings. There is also, however, an affinity in the general concept of both these decorative masterpieces: in both Rome and Mantua there is an obvious intention to increase the ideal weight of the whole structure. But Mantegna's frescoes seem to have suggested to a great number of artists an infinite variety of interpretations. The most amazing are not to be found in the harshness of expression of the Ferrarese and of Lombards such as Butinone, in the extravagance and fantasy of Urs Graf, or in the ornate wood-carvings of Michael Pacher and the Flemish pseudo-humanists like Barnard van Orley. They are rather in the battle scenes and orgies of ancient gods as represented by the Venetian painters of the Cinquecento and in their chromatic compositions. In the same way as the Eremitani *Assumption* inspired Titian's treatment of the theme in the Church of the Frari in Venice—for Titian had studied Mantegna's work in Padua in 1519 if not before—so did the illusion of the circular balustrade on the ceiling of the *Camera degli Sposi* (plates 99–101) anticipate the *sfondato* with its clashes of lights and hues, that was to become the highlight of Baroque painting.

Mantegna transformed the vault of this chamber at Padua into a precious casket of hammered metal: he reduced the shadows of the corbels by means of low reliefs which blend with the emperors, festoons, ribbons, and admirable cherubs supporting the medallions. Although one can easily detect the touch of Mantegna's assistants in several places (especially the lunettes), every detail nonetheless reflects the absolute static quality of the scenes portraying the Gonzaga, as seen within the imaginary porticos represented along two of the walls. The portraits are coldly and analytically studied, but any satirical intention is concealed by the calm and measured attitude of the figures—even in the case of grotesque characters such as the woman-dwarf. As a result, the easy everyday life of the small Mantuan court acquires an extraordinary dignity. Each feature, furthermore, though heraldically conceived, remains perfectly natural.

In the scene in which Lodovico greets his son (plate 80) the Mantuan countryside so accurately portrayed in the *Death of the Virgin* (plate 76) reappears, but this time with walls and towers, stony terraces, castles and fantastic trees (plates 92, 94, 96, 98). The suspended gestures of the figures (plates 87 and 90), the improbable volumes in the background, the mysterious pattern of light seen through the rocks (plates 96 and 98), give the scene a feeling of suspense. Something fatal is about to happen. An exception to Mantegna's normally expressionless figures are the three girls looking down from the *trompe l'œil* parapet (plate 100), though not in the case of the heads of the two women on their right, one closely resembling Ludovico's wife, Barbara of Brandenburg, and the other a handsome negress (plate 101). In these two faces the balance of volumes is enhanced by the counterpoint of colors, a principle common to many *Sacre Conversazioni* Mantegna painted toward the end of his life. (One that was appreciated by his imitators who found it a good excuse for repeating the artist's typical faces again and again.) Such is the case in the *Adoration of the Magi*: the closest copy of Mantegna's manner is to be found in Northampton (plate 169). This applies, too, to the recently restored *Madonna and Child with the Infant St John and Saints* in Turin (plate 129), a study of the balance of volumes within a horizontal rectangle; or again of the *Madonna and Child with the Infant St John and Saints* in Dresden (plate 139) and the *Holy Family with a Female Saint* in Verona (plate 143), both probably executed in the last decade of the fifteenth century, when Mantegna's activities were coming to an end.

Documents do not tell us much about Mantegna's work in this period. He carried out routine activities at the Court of Mantua, and was laying the foundations of a museum-villa for himself and his family. In 1484 he had been invited to Rome but did not go, which leads us to conclude that in his capacity as Court Painter he had to perform more duties than is suggested by the evidence of his work.

The admiration for Mantegna's drawings for the *Triumphs of Caesar* (plates 113–121) must have been considerable, because they began to be imitated and copied even before they were completed. The unusual theme of an absolutely classical epic appealed to the ambition of an age that was becoming more and more culture-conscious as reconstruction and reinterpretation of history was fast replacing the use of the classics for the mere benefit of preceptors and theological moralists. We know that the *Triumphs* were interrupted in 1488 for over a year when Mantegna was in the Vatican, working for Pope Innocent VIII, but it could hardly be claimed, as some critics have, that following his visit to Rome the artist lost interest in antiquity. True, in his letters from the Eternal City he mostly described the odd people he had met and said little or nothing about the architectural marvels he must have seen. On the other hand, his collection of ancient pieces must have been enriched to a considerable degree by his excursion. Andrea's admiration for Rome and its former greatness, born from a study of ancient writers and fed by his contacts with Paduan scholars who had promoted the humanistic Renaissance in the Papal

Court, could not possibly have faded at the sight of those formidable ruins, half-buried though they were under medieval buildings. Rather, he retained his vision of a triumphant Caesar.

It is hard to believe that those great works of art, now hanging irreparably damaged on the walls of Hampton Court Palace, were intended to decorate a stage, but that is a significant indication of taste at the time of their execution. The admiration with which they were greeted was equalled by the indifference with which they were preserved for posterity by the disorderly Gonzagas—at whose court magnificent pageantry went hand in hand with avarice, often to the detriment of their Court Painter. Mantegna must have thought highly of his *Triumphs* for he had planned to make them the background for his archaeological collection in the museum-villa (one should add here that the greats of that day passing through Mantua never failed to express great interest in its construction). The building in fact became a landmark in the evolution of taste for the classical architecture of the Cinquecento.

By the end of the fifteenth century research into the fields of chiaroscuro, tonality, and light had changed the extent of the artist's emotional participation in his work. At this point, Mantegna's *Triumph* marked a revolutionary step in iconography. For him, of course, this was merely a logical development of what he had previously been doing, a freer and more complete expression of what he believed an artist's mission to be. The revelation and exaltation of Caesar's triumphant greatness is the result of extremely intelligent theatrical direction: the procession is raised to the level of the spectator's eye and occasionally silhouetted against the sky, thus creating a foreground of powerful masses behind which one can imagine the great crowds. Above the marching figures and their forest of trumpets and pikes, we sense the immensity of space. The size of the pageant is increased by its division into episodes which, however, are not self-contained but overlapping—so that in spite of the pilasters which originally framed each episode, the impression was that of a continuous procession. Though intent on an evocation of antiquity, Mantegna nevertheless endowed each figure with the gestures that were essential for the balance of his scenes, and by these gestures he individualized each character. By doing this he avoided the effect of some kind of anonymous commemoration, so typical of the work of his imitators. By avoiding emphasis he achieved solemnity. The spectator, though remaining outside the scene and feeling only admiration, watches the concise, rigid volumes of chariots, spoils of art and war, busts, helms, shields and human anatomies filing past, but does not smell the dust, the sweat, the flesh—the horror of war. He experiences none of the feelings unleashed by conquered humanity in the *Triumphs* of Rubens (which were inspired by Mantegna), because no feelings are demanded of him but admiration: Mantegna's humanity is, as always, polished marble. It is an example that need not move us, because it derives from sublime sentiments and therefore is created for only one purpose: the solemn presentation of a majestic triumph.

Perhaps the monochrome canvas of *Tarquinius and the Sibyl* in Cincinnati (plate 112) was painted while Mantegna was preparing the *Triumphs of Caesar*. He certainly painted numerous fine monochromes in the Vatican Chapel of Innocent VIII, and in the adjoining sacristy he devised ornamental motifs generally popular with *intarsia* decorators. He represented a *trompe l'œil* cupboard filled with articles for celebrating Mass. These works were later destroyed on the orders of Pope Pius VI, but their description leaves no doubt as to the love and care the artist took in such still-life exercises. The paintings inside the chapel itself, and its ceiling decorated with foliage, must have been the basic concept for the *Madonna della Vittoria* altarpiece (plates 132–133), executed afterwards, and of which Mantegna's followers left a poor imitation on the ceiling of the Burial Chapel of Sant'Andrea in Mantua. There the young Correggio, perhaps, painted the four Evangelists seated in the corbels, yet another motif from Rome. And it was certainly Correggio who, in the *Chamber of the Badessa* in San Paolo in Parma, executed a lively decoration of foliage, cherubs and monochromes, very reminiscent of the *Camera degli Sposi* in Mantua, and a much more lively, intelligent interpretation of Mantegna's idea than the uninspired figures in Sant' Andrea.

Vasari tells how while in Rome Mantegna also painted the *Madonna of the Stonecutters*, now in the Uffizi (plates 122–125). But some critics maintain that it was executed earlier, during one of the artist's journeys in Tuscany. Vasari's description of the painting is accurate, with the exception that the Child, whom he describes as being asleep, has his eyes open. Mantegna rendered the workers in the background with extraordinary detail (plate 125). This is indeed one of his most breath-taking pictures, wholly steeped in the rosy shade of the enormous rock of conglomerated crystals framing the group of Mother and Child, with light falling delicately on the glittering pebbles at the Virgin's feet.

Returning from Rome, Mantegna completed the *Triumphs of Caesar*, then began working in Marmirolo Castle. Meanwhile, Marquis Francesca Gonzaga, Lodovico's heir, had married Isabella d'Este (the artist could not attend the wedding because at the time he had been ill in Rome).

Mantegna's relationship with Isabella was probably difficult. In Lombardy a new star was rising—Leonardo da Vinci—and perhaps she would have preferred to have as her court painter, a portraitist able to reproduce the live texture of faces by means of his *sfumato* technique. In his letters Mantegna had repeatedly stressed how important quiet, thought, and frequent sittings were so that he could paint his fierce portraits. But although Isabella continued to praise his inventiveness and the merits of his compositions (which she considered superior to those of Giovanni Bellini and Perugino), she preferred the portrait techniques of Giovanni Santi.

On his return to Mantua from Rome Mantegna seemed to become even more austere. The pervading softness of Venetian tints, the devaluation of Leonardo's works after frequent copying, the increasing influence of the Umbrians and Perugino seemed to bring out the more controversial side of his nature. At this time the theme of *Sacra Conversazione* recurs more frequently among his elaborate compositions. In 1485 he painted a *Virgin and Child with Other Figures* for Eleanor of Aragon. This might conceivably be the painting now in the Galleria Sabauda in Turin (plate 129), though this work has additions which are not by Mantegna. At any rate the balanced symmetry of the composition and the silence that seems to envelop the swelling volumes suggest a much later date. A Ferrara inventory of 1493 lists a "Madonna and Child with Seraphim" which might be the *Virgin and Child with Cherubim* in the Brera, stylistically very close to the *Madonna della Vittoria* (plate 132). The Brera painting recalls a theme often repeated by Jacopo Bellini and later by Giovanni in the *Madonna with Red Cherubim* in the Venice Accademia. Mantegna's work, however, goes back to the ancient iconic conception of the Byzantines and it shows the gigantic and obsessive imagery of that period.

I do not think, moreover, that the *Madonna della Vittoria* induces much tender admiration in the spectator. The altarpiece was carried triumphantly into a chapel especially built for it in the Church of Santa Maria della Vittoria, erected in Mantua after the Battle of Fornovo, on July 6, 1496. Mary's beauty is obvious, and the bower is very attractive with its foliage, fruits, birds, and precious beads painted with a realism that would have put Crivelli to shame. But the picture's almost macabre, mysterious immobility emanates from the great coral root hanging in the center, so cold that it takes the color out of everything else.

We proceed now to the subversion of spatial order that makes the Madonna in the altarpiece for Santa Maria in Organo at Verona (now in the Castello Sforzesco, Milan) appear enormous rather than magnificent. From the *Madonna della Vittoria* to this work was a short step, but indicative of a new violence of expression. The vision of the Virgin is taken back into the distance within a *mandorla* of cherubs, and four stalagmitic Saints (plate 137) form a barrier between the vision and the spectator. The flora, painted with paranoic botanical precision, is most unreal, and the very plausible group of singing angels below loses credibility because of the impossible perspective in which it is placed.

The concept of the *Virgin and Child with St John the Baptist and Mary Magdalen* in London (plate 134) is similar. The Virgin is the prototype of Correggio's sweet Madonnas, and yet a web of harsh luminosity surrounding the pinks and blues makes each form impenetrable. The heavily stressed facial mime, exaggerated gestures and the ruthless, precise definition become almost stentorian here. It is as if the artist, afraid that his sacred conception should slip into the realms of mythology, tried to make each of his figures as solid as he possibly could.

Another work in the National Gallery, the *Holy Family with St John* (plate 140) fits into the pattern of Mantegna's last works. So damaged that the Virgin's gesture was difficult to interpret when the painting was last restored, this picture reveals a definite intention to present forms as visual symbols—indeed as hieroglyphs. The elliptical mouth of the well on which Christ is standing has the function of connecting the figures of Redemption, St John and Mary, above whom the protective expanded volume of Joseph's head gazes outward. All scaling in space is carefully avoided, as if the majestic presence of Christ the Redeemer had compelled the artist to portray his figures frontally. Only the Mother, whose face is shadowed by Christ—yet another symbol?—is seen in profile and she is very similar to one of the angels in the altarpiece in the Castello Sforzesco (plate 136). But the two children are not completely expressionless; rather than stout little boys they recall herculean dwarfs, such is their purposeful seriousness.

Mantegna may be accused of lack of feeling in the works painted for the studio of Isabella Gonzaga and which are now in the Louvre. Only the polished and fine execution—in so far as it is by Mantegna—prevents the so-called *Parnassus* (plate 150) from being dismissed as a pretentious collection of ill-defined and distorted poses. Clearly the moral fable did not appeal to the artist's imagination and so could not form part of a decorative scheme. The classical motifs represented with such obvious effort overpower and conceal the landscape, which is as beautiful and fascinating as ever and forms some lovely small scenes. Even more laborious is the *Triumph of Virtue* (plate 151), in which the artist's realism becomes ponderous, the invention forced and his lyrical participation disappears altogether, although here, too, a magnificent valley is depicted in the background. These works were executed respectively before 1497 and between 1501 and 1502. Mantegna was probably reluctant to continue this commission because in the last years of his life he did no more than trace a few details of the fable of *Comus, the God of Revelry* (plates 152–153) which was later entirely painted by Costa.

Yet in these last years Mantegna also painted the monochrome in the National Gallery, London, generally known as the *Triumph of Scipio* (plates 144–145). Longhi's essay notes that this work and two other monochromes in London representing *Tuccia* and *Sophonisba* (plate 146) were to have formed part of one whole decorative scheme to which Giovanni Bellini had already contributed the *Continence of Scipio* now in the Kress Collection. Certainly it is here, rather than in Isabella Gonzaga's *Allegories*, that Mantegna's late artistry is more clearly to be seen. In these works, in the admirable relationship created between the background and the figures, one finds again—though with more detachment—the intensity of *Samson and Delilah* (plate 147) also in London, a painting that was probably executed during the artist's stay in Rome. Perhaps Mantegna composed no other picture so domestic and yet at the same time so fateful.

The closing years of the century seem to have been crucial for the artist, torn as he was between plain narration and the need to make his paintings cry out. This dilemma is well illustrated in two works, the *Madonna della Vittoria* (plate 132) and the *Madonna and Child with Four Saints* in the Castello Sforzesco (plate 135), and even better so in *Christ Seated on a Sarcophagus* in Copenhagen (plate 141) and the *St Sebastian* in the Ca' d'Oro in Venice (plate 142). The bold self-confidence of Mantegna's figures was now becoming a violent cry of despair: his fight against sorrow is ever present in the contracted profiles. Not that this made his works less effective.

Indeed, they were even more disturbing than Tura's *St James della Marca* who could be the brother of Mantegna's *St Sebastian*. In common with many of the noblest minds of the early Cinquecento, Mantegna had understood that in those difficult, insecure times, the austere and powerful conception of man as a maker of history, so beloved by the Humanists, could only exist in theory. The flame of ancient faith was flickering and being replaced by sterile erudition. Mantegna would never have succumbed to this and that is why, in his last works, he strove desperately to impart new life into what were now old formal conventions. That is why his images lost their former self-assurance and betray the consciousness of an artist who must once again explain and justify his authority more strongly than ever.

How could Andrea Mantegna embark on a new search for the value of man within the relativity of Nature? How could he become interested—as Leonardo did—in scientific enlightenment? For him the balance between ideas and sentiments had vanished. This is the anguished cry of his last paintings. His *St Sebastian* looks like a Samson tensing his muscles before destroying the temple. The artist's personal conflict explodes somewhere between the commanding immobility of his volumes and the violent breaks in his outlines. This is the period when he drew a *Judith and the Negress*, now at the Uffizi and previously owned by Vasari who described it. Each line in this drawing seems to shout in horror and the figure of Judith herself, slowly revolving around a solid axis, is given unprecedented energy, a new responsibility for the revenge she had just accomplished. All Mantegna's previous treatments of this theme suggested a fatalistic surrender to the inevitable. Not here.

Another very great and famous work was also painted in Mantegna's last years. This is the *Dead Christ* in the Brera (plates 130–131). The merit of the work, rather than in the famous foreshortening of the figure of Christ, is to be found in the leaden dusky tones resulting from the very thin tempera, which eliminate any anatomical emphasis. The presence of the dead Christ and the grief of those who mourn are expressed on the same plane and with the same intensity. This composition is peculiar to Mantegna's last period: the figures of St John and Mary (plate 131) fill the space vertically, a device already used in the *Holy Family with St John* (plate 140) and which was to be used again in the *Madonna and Child with the Infant St John and Saints* in Dresden (plate 139) and in the *Holy Family with a Female Saint* in Verona (plate 143). Ultimately this device was to become typical of the Mannerists of the early Cinquecento. But in the Brera masterpiece there is a sublimity of genuine invention that nothing can rival. Its alleged "model" found by Tietze in the United States (plate 168) seems to me to be rather an improved copy, so minutely faithful is it to the original.

The *Dead Christ*, the *Triumph of Scipio* and the *St Sebastian* in Venice, were in Mantegna's home at the time of his death. In them was his spiritual testament: the *Triumph of Scipio* is the best of his classical paintings, and Giovanni Bellini, who collaborated with him in this commission, worked with care, for Mantegna was the acknowledged master in such subjects. Mantegna's pupils were to work with Giulio Romano on the splendid mythological decoration of the Palazzo del Te in Mantua. The Grecian grace of gestures and drapery which he had rediscovered would reappear mainly in the stuccos of Primaticcio who, however times having changed, was to seek his inspiration not from the heroes of old but from a concept of elegance for elegance's sake. The silent poetry of the foreshortened Christ marks a moment of Mantegna's ultimate confessional, but the rhythm of his composition, aimed at stilling all emotion by exhausting it by the very effort of expression, reveals a moral crisis. Of course he expressed it directly, that is, the torment of his art, and in so doing Andrea Mantegna bequeathed his successors a number of solutions which—seen as mere exaggeration of forms— were to pave the way, and potentially a very fertile one, for the Mannerists.

# BIOGRAPHICAL NOTES

1431. Mantegna's probable birth-date because of the inscription he put on an altarpiece (now lost) which he painted in 1448 for the Church of Santa Sofia in Padua. The inscription was recorded by Scardeone and Vasari. That he worked at the altarpiece is confirmed by a document discovered by Lazzarini. All the documents and ancient biographies concerning Mantegna confirm this date.

1441–5, NOVEMBER 6. During this period Mantegna—officially described as the son of Master Franzesco Squarzon, painter—was made a member of the Guild of Paduan painters. From the records of the lawsuit that followed we may assume that Squarcione adopted Mantegna not later than 1442.

1448, JANUARY 26. Squarcione and Mantegna agree to a compromise. After this date the artist appears to have become independent and free to dispose of his earnings.

1448, MAY 16. Niccoló Pizzolo and Andrea Mantegna, who is represented by his brother because he is still a minor, sign a contract with the widow of Antonio Ovetari, in which they promise to paint one half of the family chapel in the Church of the Eremitani at Padua. The sum of 700 gold ducats to finance the enterprise, the instructions concerning the decoration and the amount of money for the chapel's maintenance had been decided by Antonio Ovetari before his death, between January 5, 1443 and April 22, 1446. One half of the sum was to go to Antonio Vivarini and Giovanni d' Alemagna, who were entrusted with the decoration of the other wall and the vaulting of the chapel.

1448, JULY 15. Pizzolo and Mantegna receive a first payment of 50 ducats for their work in the Ovetari Chapel.

1448, SEPTEMBER 5. Litigation occurs between Squarcione and Mantegna concerning the valuation of the paintings by Pietro da Milano in the Church of San Giacomo at Padua.

1448, OCTOBER 16. Bartolomeo, a baker, pays Mantegna 40 ducats for the altarpiece of Santa Sofia. This work, according to Scardeone, was inscribed: ANDREA MANTINEA PAT. AN. SEPTEM ET DECEM NATUS SUA MANU PINXIT MCCCCXLVIII.

1449, MAY 23. The artist is in Ferrara where he paints the portrait of Lionello d'Este, and on the reverse he paints the portrait of Folco di Villafora. This work has been lost.

1449, SEPTEMBER 27. In the course of an arbitration, Francesco Morosini declares the partnership between Pizzolo and Mantegna to be broken, and allots them separate tasks. It appears that Pizzolo had already begun to paint the apse and cupola of the chapel and the figures of God the Father and St James. Mantegna had to complete the other three figures of SS Peter, Paul, and Christopher. Pizzolo was to decorate the right side of the arch and Mantegna the left, in addition to five compartments of the episodes from the *Life of St James*. Pizzolo was instructed to paint the compartment nearest to the altar and was put in sole charge of the terracotta altarpiece. Documents state that the artists had already received more than they were due for the work they had done, and were therefore instructed to complete their respective tasks. In case of the death of one of them, the other was to receive a sum of money equivalent to the amount of work that he would have to complete. This in fact happened, as Pizzolo died and Mantegna had to paint the *Martyrdom of St James*. The right wall, which was to have been decorated by Giovanni d'Alemagna and Vivarini, was handed over, when Giovanni died in 1450, to the new partnership established between Mantegna and Ansuino da Forlì. In 1451, the two artists received some payments and in that same year similar payments were made to Ansuino and Bono da Ferrara. In 1452 Pizzolo received what was perhaps his last payment.

1452, JULY 21. This date appears upon the lunette of the main entrance of the Church of San Antonio in Padua. The fresco has now been transferred to the Museo Antoniano (see plate 12).

1453, AUGUST 10. Mantegna undertakes to paint the *St Luke Polyptych*—now in the Brera Gallery, Milan—for the Church of Santa Giustina in Padua. He was paid in full by November, 1454.

1453, FEBRUARY 23. Jacopo Bellini withdraws some funds from the School of San Giovanni Evangelista in Venice, intending to set them aside for the dowry of his daughter Nicolosa.

1454, FEBRUARY 25. Jacopo withdraws more funds from the School of San Giovanni Evangelista for the dowry of his daughter who by then had probably already become Mantegna's wife.

1454. This date appears on the Sant' Eufemia panel, now in Naples.

1455, NOVEMBER 28. Mantegna instructs his legal adviser to request the sum of 400 ducats from Squarcione as compensation for the works and services he rendered during the six years of Squarcione's tutorship.

1456, JANUARY 2. The compromise stipulated between Mantegna and Squarcione in 1448 is declared nul and void, but the litigation between them goes on for more than a year.

1457, JANUARY 5. Mantegna writes to Marquis Lodovico Gonzaga accepting his invitation to go to Mantua as his Court Painter. He asks, however, that before going he may be allowed to finish the Polyptych for the Church of San Zeno in Verona.

44

1457, FEBRUARY 14. Pietro da Milano claims that he can tell that the frescoes on the left wall of the Ovetari Chapel and the *Assumption* in the apse were painted by Mantegna, even though he did not witness in person the work in the Chapel. He states that a painter's hand, especially if he is a great master, can always be recognized by his colleagues. He states, furthermore, that in spite of the widow Ovetari's complaints (she was encouraged by Squarcione), Mantegna could not have painted all the twelve Apostles below the *Assumption* without damaging the general artistic effect. The following day Squarcione stated that, had Mantegna taken the trouble to paint them a little smaller, all twelve Apostles could have fit in below the *Assumption*.

1457, NOVEMBER 27; 1458, April 15, November 14, December 26; 1459, February 2, March 14, May 4, June 28, June 29: dates of letters written by Lodovico Gonzaga to Mantegna, to the papal protonotary, Gregorio Correr, and to the Mayor of Padua, in order to hurry Mantegna to Mantua. The artist is definitely recorded as living in Mantua in the summer of 1460, but perhaps he had already paid a few odd visits to the city because on May 14, 1459, the Marquis informed him that the palace's chapel "has been completed in accordance with your instructions." On January 30, 1459, Mantegna, who was now called a *familiaris* of the Gonzaga Court was authorized to have a coat of arms of his own and the motto "par un desir."

1463, JANUARY 1. Felice Feliciano dedicates to Mantegna a collection

of ancient epigraphs now in the Capitolare Library in Verona.

1463, FEBRUARY 19. Mantegna is busy directing the decoration of Cavriana Castle where his drawings were faithfully translated into frescoes by Samuele da Tradate, probably the son of Jacopino. Documents dated March 7 and 12, 1464, testify that this procedure was normally followed.

1464, April 26. Having stayed for several months at Goito, Mantegna writes to Gonzaga complaining that the frames for the panels destined for the chapel of the Mantuan castle are not ready. The panels were to have been put in the chapel at the end of the month.

1464, SEPTEMBER 23. Felice Feliciano writes in the account of an archaeological expedition which he undertook with Mantegna, the painter, Samuele da Tradate, and Giovanni Antenorea, an engineer. On this occasion the three men gave each other Roman consular titles.

1465, DECEMBER 5. The Mantuan Court orders preparations to be made for a tapestry designed by Mantegna.

1466, MARCH 1. Lodovico Ganzaga writes to his wife, Barbara of Brandenburg, instructing her to have a portrait by Mantegna copied.

1466, JULY 5. Mantegna is in Florence, probably in connection with the tribune of the Annunziata which Gonzaga had promised to finance and Leon Battista Alberti to design and construct.

45

1467, JULY 3. Mantegna goes to Pisa where he has been consulted about the decoration of the cemetery.

1468, JULY 27. Mantegna informs Gonzaga that he has begun to paint a "history of Limbo."

1469, FEBRUARY 2. Marsilio Andreani, Lodovico Gonzaga's secretary, writes to the Marchioness Barbara informing her of Mantegna's desire to be made a Count. In fact the artist, when he called at the Vatican, signed himself: "Comes Palatinus."

1469, JULY 11. Lodovico Gonzaga instructs Mantegna to draw two "hens from India" for a tapestry.

1470–71. Mantegna's presence in Mantua is documented by correspondence between the Marquis and himself mainly concerning the artist's quarrels with several people.

1471, OCTOBER 25. Lodovico Gonzaga orders that three lots of walnut oil be sent to Mantegna, probably for polishing the leatherwork in the *Camera degli Sposi*, which Lodovico was anxious to see completed.

1472, JULY 18. Cardinal Francesco Gonzaga writes to his father Lodovico asking him to send Mantegna to him to examine his collection of precious stones and bronzes. On September 21 the artist was still with the Cardinal in Porretta.

1472. Mantegna apparently helped to plan the courtyard of the Mantua castle. This was executed by Fancelli but designed by Lodovico Gonzaga himself.

1472, NOVEMBER 20. Gonzaga decrees that Mantegna be given 800 ducats to buy a piece of land at Buscoldo. On May 13, 1478, however, the artist complains that he has not yet received the whole sum and the Marquis apologizes and points out that his financial situation is very difficult. In the following years many judicial disputes are recorded between Mantegna and some of his neighbors and collaborators, who complained to the Marquis of his quarrelsome nature. Gonzaga always protected the artist.

1477, JULY 6. The Marquis would like Mantegna to paint his portrait and those of his family while they are all away from Mantua. The artist explains his reluctance by saying that a portrait from life needs meditation and an opportunity to study the model.

1478, OCTOBER 16. After Lodovico's death his son and heir Federico Gonzaga writes to Mantegna asking him to go and stay with him in Gonzaga. The artist, however, is ill and cannot travel. Federico showed Mantegna greater consideration than his father.

1480, MAY 11. Marquis Federico asks the physician, Gherardo da Verona, to look after Mantegna's son who is seriously ill. The boy's death soon afterwards affected Mantegna for the rest of his life.

1481, APRIL 24. The artist goes to Marmirolo to give instructions to the engineer, Giovanni da Padova.

1483, FEBRUARY. On more than one occasion Mantegna instructs the goldsmith, Gian Marco Cavalli, about the decoration of vases and

46

drinking vessels. In the same year the artist's workshop is visited by Lorenzo the Magnificent who expresses admiration for some of Mantegna's paintings, reliefs of heads, and ancient pieces.

1483, FEBRUARY 25. Mantegna seems to be decorating yet another room in the Mantuan castle, because on this date Bishop Gonzaga explains to the Prefect of Rome, Giovanni della Rovere, that it is impossible for the artist to interrupt his work and go to Rome.

1484, AUGUST 26. Mantegna requests a subsidy from Lorenzo de' Medici for the erection of the museum-villa that he is planning for himself.

1485, NOVEMBER 6. Federico Gonzaga writes to Eleonaro of Aragon assuring her that he will have Mantegna finish a *Madonna* for her with other figures sketched by the artist and which she had particularly liked. But, despite repeated requests, on December 15 the work was still unfinished.

1486, AUGUST 26. The artist has begun the *Triumphs of Caesar* and the work is progressing rapidly.

1488, JUNE 10. Francesco Gonzaga, who succeeded his father as Lord of Mantua in 1484, presents Mantegna to Pope Innocent VIII.

1488. This date was discovered in 1961 during the restoration of the fresco of the *SS Andrew and Longinus*, attributed to Mantegna by Paccagnini, but probably executed by his pupils after his drawings.

1489, JUNE 15. Mantegna writes a long letter to Marquis Francesco in which he reports that all he receives for his work in the Chapel of Innocent VIII are his boarding expenses. This is followed by an amusing description of the brother of the Turkish Sultan, Djem, who "walks like an elephant and . . . wears on his head thirty thousand lengths of cloth!" The artist writes that he is as yet unable to draw the Turk because "his appearance keeps changing all the time and I cannot memorize it." Mantegna has recorded once again his difficulty in drawing from memory. On the other hand this letter proves how interested he was, from the psychological point of view, in his models.

1489, DECEMBER 16. Francesco Gonzaga asks the Pope to allow Mantegna to return to Mantua for the prince's marriage to Isabella d'Este. The artist, however, is ill and the Pope replies that it would be dangerous to expose *talem virum* to the risks of such a journey.

1491, OCTOBER 5. Mantegna is back in Mantua.

1492, FEBRUARY 14. Marquis Gonzaga presents Mantegna with a new gift of land, in payment for his work in the Chapel, in the *Camera degli Sposi* and for the *Triumphs of Caesar* which the artist is still painting.

1493, JANUARY 12. Isabella d'Este instructs Mantegna to paint her portrait, so that she may send it to the Countess dell' Acerra.

1493, APRIL 20. Isabella d'Este apologizes to the Countess dell' Acerra for not having sent her the portrait and explains that "it is not a good likeness." She sent the Countess another one on January 14 of the following year. The painter was Giovanni Santi.

1494. Several reports mention the *Triumphs of Caesar* which is nearly finished. Meanwhile in Marmirolo, Mantegna directs the work of his son Francesco, together with Francesco Bonsignori, Tondo, who is said to be a specialist at painting exotic figurines, and Benesella.

1496, JULY 6. Sigismondo Gonzaga reports to Marquis Francesco that a procession has taken place to commemorate the Battle of Fornovo and that the *Madonna della Vittoria*, painted by Mantegna, has been exhibited in public.

1496. The monks of Santa Maria in Organo at Verona send several gifts to Mantegna who is painting a canvas for their high altar. The painting, now in Castello Sforzesco, Milan, is dated August 15, 1497. (See plate 135.)

1497, JULY 3. Alberto da Bologna writes to Isabella d'Este in Ferrara that a painting by Mantegna (*Parnassus*) has been placed in her study.

1499. Mantegna evaluates some paintings in Ferrara.

1500. The artist informs the Prior of Santa Maria in Vado that he does not have the time to paint a *Madonna* or a *St Jerome*.

1501, FEBRUARY 13. Sigismondo Cantelmo, describing a pageant held at the Court of Mantua, refers to the *Triumphs of Caesar*, used for decorating the stage and

to the *Triumph of Petrarch* on the parapet of the stage. He says that both works are by Mantegna.

1504, MARCH 1. Mantegna makes his will and testament in which he bequeaths 200 ducats to the Chapel of the Church of Sant' Andrea in Mantua.

1504, JULY 6. Lorenzo da Pavia reports that Giovanni Bellini has "diligently completed," because of respect for Andrea Mantegna, a painting which is to be part of a group of pictures devised and painted by Mantegna.

1505, JANUARY 1. Pietro Bembo tells Isabella d'Este how much he admires Mantegna.

1506, JANUARY 13. Mantegna has been seriously ill—he probably had a stroke—and writes to Isabella telling her that his financial situation is so bad that he is prepared to sell his beloved bust of Empress Faustina. The sale, which took place the following August, fetched 100 ducats.

1506, SEPTEMBER 15. Francesco Mantegna writes to Marquis Gonzaga who is in Perugia, telling him of his father's death. This occurred the previous Sunday, on September 13 at 7 p.m.

1506, OCTOBER 2. Lodovico Mantegna acknowledges his father's bequest of 200 ducats for the Chapel of Sant'Andrea. Among the paintings left in his father's workshop Lodovico recalls: "A foreshortened figure of Christ; the work about Scipio Cornelius begun for Francesco Cornaro; a St Sebastian and the two paintings which are to go to his chapel."

# MANTEGNA'S PAINTINGS

### Plate 1

HEAD OF A COLOSSUS. *Fresco. Formerly in Padua, Church of the Eremitani, on the left side of the arch leading into the apse of the Ovetari Chapel (the maximum measurements of which are: length 1110; width 885).** Probably a self-portrait of Mantegna who, as a result of the lawsuit of September 27, 1449, was commissioned to paint this head and the frescoes on the left wall; the right wall was left to Pizzolo. Destroyed by a bomb on March 11, 1944.

### Plate 2a

ST PETER. *Fresco. Formerly in Padua, Church of Eremitani, the apse, veiling, spandrels of the Ovetari Chapel.* The lawsuit of 1449 decreed that this figure and the two following ones (plates 2b and 3), all begun by Mantegna, should be completed and decorated by him, while Pizzolo was to finish *St James* and *God the Father.* Before the case was published by Rigoni in 1927 these frescoes were generally attributed to Pizzolo, but in 1914, Adolfo Venturi stated that Mantegna had contributed at least the figure of *St Christopher.* Longhi (*Vita Artistica,* 1926) pointed out that the whole apsidal decoration was in Mantegna's manner. Destroyed by a bomb on March 11, 1944.

### Plate 2b

ST PAUL. See comment on plate 2a.

### Plate 3

ST CHRISTOPHER. See comment on plate 2a.

### Plate 4

THE CALLING OF JAMES AND JOHN. *Fresco. Formerly in Padua, Church of the Eremitani, left wall of the Ovetari Chapel.* This is the first episode from the *Life of St James* (Matthew IV, 21–2). On the left is Christ between SS Peter and Andrew who have been called shortly before. Before the publication of the 1449 lawsuit Crowe and Cavalcaselle thought Mantegna's work could be seen at least in the design of the fresco. Michiel attributed the execution to Mantegna and so did Kristeller.

Adolfo Venturi—who attributed this and the following scene to Pizzolo—observed that they were in some form correlated to the corresponding scenes on the opposite wall which, in his view, were painted by Ansuino da Forli. In 1926, Longhi ascribed their design to Mantegna. Fiocco noted the influence of Tuscan sculpture in the decorative elements and that of Lippi in the coloring. Destroyed by a bomb on March 11, 1944.

### Plate 5

ST JAMES EXPELLING THE DEMONS. See comment on plate 4.

### Plate 6

ST JAMES BAPTIZING HERMO-GENES. *Fresco. Formerly in Padua, Church of the Eremitani, left wall, middle row, Ovetari Chapel.* An episode from the *Golden Legend.* A number of payments received by Mantegna in 1451,

* All dimensions are given in centimeters.

and recorded a short time before those made out to Ansuino and Bono da Ferrara, are probably related to this and the following scenes.

Before the "Book of Accounts" of Ovetari Chapel was found (Rigoni, 1948) these frescoes were believed to have been painted at a somewhat later date. It seems hardly possible that the *Martyrdom of St Christopher*, on the opposite wall, was also finished by 1451, as assumed by E. Rigoni and E. Tietze-Conrat. Critics unanimously agreed that this fresco revealed an awareness of Donatello's innovations in visual art and even more so in Piero della Francesca. They also saw a parallel with the drawings of Jacopo Bellini. Destroyed by a bomb on March 11, 1944.

Plate 7

ST JAMES BEFORE HEROD AGRIPPA. *Fresco. Formerly in Padua, Church of the Eremitani, left wall, middle row, Ovetari Chapel.* This episode is also taken from the *Golden Legend*, and is an intelligent reconstruction in which each figure has definite individual importance. A. Venturi observed that "the composition is dominated by the artist's love for antiquity." Destroyed, as were all the frescoes in the Ovetari Chapel, by a bomb on March 11, 1944.

Plate 8

ST JAMES BAPTISING HERMO-GENES. Detail: spectators and decorations on the upper right.

Plate 9

ST JAMES BAPTISING HERMO-GENES. Detail: the main figures.

Plate 10

ST JAMES BEFORE HEROD AGRIPPA. Detail: bust of warrior on the left.

Plate 11

ST JAMES BEFORE HEROD AGRIPPA. Detail: bust of officer on the right.

Plate 12

SS ANTHONY AND BERNARDINO HOLDING THE MONOGRAM OF CHRIST IN A WREATH. *Frescoed lunette (base 316). Padua, Museo Antoniano.* Originally on the tympanum above the main entrance of the Santo in Padua. Transferred to the museum during the First World War. The circular inscription reads: IN NOMINE IESV OMNE GENUFLECTA-TUR CELESTIVM TERESTRIUM ET INFERNORUM. The base is inscribed: ANDREAS MANTEGNA OPTIMO FAVENTE NVMINE PERFECIT MCCCCLII XI KAL. SEXTIL. The lunette was damaged long ago and restored in the seventeenth century by Pietro Liberi who repainted the head of St Anthony. The fresco was restored again in 1769.

# THE ST LUKE POLYPTYCH

## (Plates 13–21)

Plate 13

THE ST LUKE POLYPTYCH. *Panel, 178 × 227. Milan, Brera Gallery.* In the lower row, at the center, is St Luke (whom some critics believe is St Matthew because of some wording in the contract for the commission); at the left are SS Scolastica and

Prosdocimus; at the right are SS Benedict and Giustina. In the upper row, at the center, is Christ with the Virgin and St John; at the left, SS Daniel and Jerome; at the right, SS Augustine and Sebastian. The Polyptych was originally in the Chapel of St Luke in the Church of Santa

Giustina in Padua, for which it was commissioned on August 10, 1453 and completed in November, 1454 (the date of the final payments). The original frame was by Maestro Guglielmo and signed—falsely, in the opinion of Scardeone—by Mantegna. It was destroyed by lightning in the eighteenth century (Moschini).

The frame "gave the painting and its gold background—chosen, undoubtedly, by the donor—the splendid unity that we see in Vivarini's Venetian polyptychs" (Fiocco) and had probably been designed by Mantegna himself, as was the case with the *San Zeno Altarpiece* in Verona.

### Plate 14
THE ST LUKE POLYPTYCH. Detail: head of the Virgin.

### Plate 15
THE ST LUKE POLYPTYCH. Detail: head of St John.

### Plate 16
THE ST LUKE POLYPTYCH. The main section with the figure of St Luke.

### Color Plate I
THE MARTYRDOM OF ST JAMES. Detail of plate 23: horseman.

### Plate 17
THE ST LUKE POLYPTYCH. Christ.

### Plate 18a
THE ST LUKE POLYPTYCH. St Scolastica.

### Plate 18b
THE ST LUKE POLYPTYCH. St Prosdocimus.

### Plate 19a
THE ST LUKE POLYPTYCH. St Benedict.

### Plate 19b
THE ST LUKE POLYPTYCH. St Giustina.

### Plate 20
THE ST LUKE POLYPTYCH. SS Daniel and Jerome.

### Plate 21
THE ST LUKE POLYPTYCH. SS Augustine and Sebastian.

### Plate 22
ST JAMES HEALING THE CRIPPLE. *Fresco. Formerly in Padua, Church of the Eremitani, left wall, lower row, Ovetari Chapel.* One of the episodes that, according to the *Golden Legend,* occurred before the Saint's martyrdom. The inscription in the medallion on the central pilaster, L. VITRVVIVS / CERDO ARC / HITETUS, was apparently directly copied by Mantegna from the Arco dei Gavi in Verona—destroyed in 1805. It varies with other known readings. The execution of the middle and lower row of frescoes has led some critics to believe that Mantegna's progress toward establishing his linear perspective from the eye-level of the spectator was interrupted. In Fiocco's opinion this was due to the artist's journey to Venice after his marriage to Nicolosa Bellini. Fiocco, moreover, describes this scene as *St James Forgiving his Jailer.* Eisler, Ragghianti, E. Rigoni, E. Tietze-Conrat, and Arslan assume that during this interval the *Martyrdom of St Christopher* was painted. This theory is rejected by Moschini, Coletti and Paccagnini. The fresco was destroyed on March 11, 1944; an ancient copy, slightly different from the original, is in the Musée Jacquemart-André in Paris.

### Plate 23
THE MARTYRDOM OF ST JAMES. *Fresco. Formerly in Padua, Church of*

the *Eremitani, left wall, lower row of the Ovetari Chapel*. Vasari, who mistook this painting for the *Martyrdom of St Christopher* (plates 36 and 37), indicates a number of portraits in the scene, and his doubtful suggestions have been accepted by some critics. (See, however, comment on plate 36.) This section was to have been painted by Pizzolo, in accordance with the 1449 lawsuit, but Mantegna executed it after his colleague's death. Therefore it should be dated at least 1454, and in any case before 1457. Crowe and Cavalcaselle and A. Venturi thought the severed head of the Saint to have been painted not by Mantegna but by an even younger assistant. The work was destroyed on March 11, 1944, and partially reassembled after the war, when its minute fragments were patiently identified and pieced together against a color photograph.

## Plate 24
ST JAMES HEALING THE CRIPPLE. Detail: main figures at the left.

## Plate 25
ST JAMES HEALING THE CRIPPLE. Detail: the architecture in the right background.

## Plate 26
ST JAMES HEALING THE CRIPPLE. Detail: head of soldier at the left.

## Plate 27
ST JAMES HEALING THE CRIPPLE. Detail: soldier pushing back the standard-bearer, at the right.

## Plate 28
THE MARTYRDOM OF ST JAMES. Detail: horseman and soldiers at the left.

## Plate 29
THE MARTYRDOM OF ST JAMES. Detail: the landscape.

## Plate 30
THE CHRIST CHILD STANDING IN A NICHE. *Panel, 70.2 × 35. Washington, D.C., National Gallery of Art, Samuel H. Kress Collection.* Formerly part of the Cook Collection at Richmond, where T. Borenius refused to acknowledge it as a work by Mantegna. Arslan supports Borenius and Kristeller assigns it to a pupil from Verona, perhaps Bonsignori. Berenson classified it as an autograph Mantegna, and so do Fiocco, E. Tietze-Conrat, and Paccagnini who date it in Mantegna's late period. Longhi, in 1926, thought it was executed before the Mantua cycle. E. Tietze-Conrat considers it may possibly be identified with "a little boy, fully clothed" mentioned in the Gonzaga di Novellare Inventory published by Campori.

## Plate 31
MADONNA AND CHILD WITH CHERUBIM. *Panel, 43.7 × 28.6. New York, Metropolitan Museum of Art.* Probably from the collection of Doctor Fusaro of Padua, where Crowe and Cavalcaselle recorded: "This panel might be called Mantegna with more propriety than any of the so-called originals at Padua." The work was later in the J. Stirling-Dyce Collection in London from which it went to the Charles Butler Collection, also in London (it has often been described as the *Butler Madonna*). Later still it became the property of Michael Friedsman of New York and was finally donated to the Metropolitan Museum in the Altman Bequest. Kristeller tentatively attributes it to Mantegna. Adolfo Venturi, Knapp, and E.

Tietze-Conrat believe this and the Berlin *Virgin and Child* (plate 69) to be derived from a Mantegna original. Berenson, Fiocco (who date it 1454), Van Marle, G. M. Richter (who date it 1450), Suida and Arslan attribute it unhesitatingly to Mantegna. Mason-Perkins and the compilers of the Metropolitan Museum's Catalogue (1940) describe the painting as presumably executed after Mantegna's design. Paccagnini suggests a joint effort by Mantegna and Giovanni Bellini at the end of the Mantua period. Gilbert notes correctly that the Virgin's face has been repainted and dates the panel in the same period as the *St Euphemia* in Naples (plate 32).

### Plate 32

ST EUPHEMIA. *Canvas, 171 × 78. Naples, Museo Nazionale di Capodimonte.* Formerly in the Museo Borgia at Velletri. The inscription at the Virgin's feet reads: OPUS ANDREAE MANTEGNAE MCCCCLIIII. The authenticity of the inscription was confirmed by restoration in 1960, and the restoration also revealed the landscape in the background and the second festoon behind the arch, previously covered by repainting.

### Color Plate II

THE AGONY IN THE GARDEN. Detail of plate 45: landscape at right.

### Plate 33

THE ASSUMPTION OF THE VIRGIN. *Detached fresco (length of base 238). Padua, Church of the Eremitani, Apse, back wall.* The fresco was detached from the wall in 1865 together with the *Martyrdom of St Christopher*. As a result both paintings escaped destruction in 1944. In the nineteenth century the composition was barbaric-

ally stretched out and consequently the figures of the Apostles disappeared behind the altar. This has now been put right, as the fresco's original measurements had fortunately survived in a print by Francesco Novelli from a drawing done by Luca Brida before the detachment. Before documents on the Ovetari Chapel were discovered (Rigoni, 1927), the *Assumption* was attributed to Pizzolo, but Crowe and Cavalcaselle would not believe that Mantegna had had no part in either this work or the lunette with the two first scenes from the *Life of St James*. Their opinion was generally accepted, particularly by Longhi who detected in this picture "the highest quality of all the works in the Chapel." In February 1457, Imperatrice Ovetari, probably encouraged by Squarcione, asked why Mantegna had not represented the full number of Apostles instead of only eight. Clearly, therefore, the work could not have been completed much before that date.

### Plate 34

THE ASSUMPTION OF THE VIRGIN. Detail: the Virgin.

### Plate 35

THE ASSUMPTION OF THE VIRGIN. Detail: the eight Apostles.

### Plate 36

THE MARTYRDOM OF ST CHRISTOPHER. First episode. *Detached fresco. Padua, Church of the Eremitani, lower row of the right wall of the Ovetari Chapel.* Detached in 1865 (see comment on plate 33), this painting consists of two combined sections separated by a column (total length of base 691). In the left scene, based on the *Golden Legend*, the archers, after several futile attempts, gaze in astonishment as their arrows change direction in mid-air, one piercing the eye of the tyrant at the window. The giant figure of the Saint, once visible on the extreme left, has almost entirely vanished. In the right-hand compartment Christopher's huge body is dragged away through the street. From a small but faithful reproduction in the Musée Jacquemart-André in Paris we know that the foreground showed the Saint's severed head. The architecture in the background is typical of the early Quattrocento, though enriched with the archaeological motifs and marble decorations of the Lombard-Venetian Renaissance. In one of the two scenes, possibly that on the left, Vasari identified Squarcione in the "Corpulent man with a spear and a sword in his hands . . . Noferi di Messer Palla Strozzi from Florence, Messer Girolamo della Valle, a most eminent physician; Messer Bonifazio Fuzimeliga, a man of law; Nicholas, the goldsmith of Pope Innocent VIII; Baldasarre from Lecce and a certain Bishop from Hungary, a man altogether witless." In the *Martyrdom of St James* (plate 23) Vasari saw a portrait of Marsilio Pazzo in the executioner. It is doubtful, however, which painting the biographer had in mind; nor is it clear whether the portraits of live models that Mantegna is said to have painted (following Squarcione's teaching) appear in the *Martyrdom of St James* or in the *Martyrdom of St Christopher*. Crowe and Cavalcaselle have observed in this fresco a softening of Mantegna's modeling due, perhaps, to the influence of the Bellini family. Indeed, they toyed with the idea that Gentile might have collaborated in the three profiles of

spectators under the tyrant's window (plate 39). The theory is interesting from a critical point of view, but lacks any foundation. M. Davies has claimed that this work may be dated later than 1449. Fiocco now supports Davies and so, apparently, does Paccagnini.

### Plate 37
THE MARTYRDOM OF ST CHRISTOPHER. Detail: section at the right. See comment on plate 36.

### Plate 38
THE MARTYRDOM OF ST CHRISTOPHER. First episode. Detail: heads of soldiers in the center. The head on the right is the alleged portrait of Squarcione.

### Plate 39
THE MARTYRDOM OF ST CHRISTOPHER. First episode. Detail: heads of spectators on the right.

### Plate 40
THE MARTYRDOM OF ST CHRISTOPHER. Second episode. Detail: the tyrant is struck by the arrow.

### Plate 41
THE MARTYRDOM OF ST CHRISTOPHER. Second episode. Detail: the window on the left and spectators.

### Plate 42
THE MARTYRDOM OF ST CHRISTOPHER. Second episode. Detail: heads on the right.

### Plate 43
THE MARTYRDOM OF ST CHRISTOPHER. Second episode. Detail: head of man with a spear on the right.

Plate 44

THE ADORATION OF THE SHEP-
HERDS. *Tempera transferred from
wood to canvas, 40 × 55.5. New York,
Metropolitan Museum of Art.* This
work was recently in the A. Rouse-
Boughton-Knight Collection, Down-
ton Castle, Herefordshire, Great
Britain, and then in Clarence H.
Mackay Collection, Roslyn, Long
Island, U.S.A. A similar subject
painted by Mantegna, in Margherita
Gonzaga's Chapel in Ferrara, was
restored in 1506–88 by Bastiano
Filippi together with a *Death of the
Virgin* and another unspecified
painting. Later the three works
passed into the collection of King
Charles I of England and the
*Adoration of the Shepherds* was sold at
Somerset House in 1650. Yet
another treatment of the same subject, from the Prince Aldobrandini
Collection, was sold by Day in London in 1800. It is impossible to say
which of the two works found its
way to Downton Castle. Crowe and
Cavalcaselle, however, saw it there
and decided that it was by a pupil
after Mantegna's drawing. Kristeller
suggests a pupil of the Paduan period
and claims that the drawings con-
nected with the painting (the *Madonna* in the Uffizi and the *Shepherds*
at Windsor Castle) are copies.
Schmarsow favors Pizzolo, and
Borenius believes that Mantegna
painted this picture when he was
working on the predella of the *San
Zeno Altarpiece*. E. Tietze-Conrat
considers it the production of a
pupil who used drawings by Mantegna and who also painted the
panel of the *Agony in the Garden* (now
at Tours) in the *San Zeno Altarpiece*.
Other critics accept the authorship
of Mantegna. Fiocco astutely noticed
a Flemish influence in this work,
especially that of Jan van Eyck.
Fiocco, however, dates the painting somewhat too early, in or about
1449.

Plate 45

THE AGONY IN THE GARDEN.
*Panel, 63 × 80. London, National
Gallery.* Formerly in the Pamphili-
Aldobrandini Collection in Rome. In
1845 it became the property of
Cardinal Fesch and passed into the
collection of Lord Northbrook in
1894. On a rock, the signature: OPVS
ANDREA MANTEGNA. Before it was
cleaned, in 1939–40, Knapp and
Fiocco had dated this work later
than 1464, and the Davies Catalogue
of the National Gallery (1951) still
suggests a dating after 1460. Crowe
and Cavalcaselle identified it with a
"smaller piece for Giacomo Marcello, in 1459." Richter (in the Cata-
log of the Northbrook Collection)
and Kristeller supported this theory.
Adolfo Venturi agrees with the
dating, which has been confirmed by
the recent cleaning. E. Tietze-
Conrat believes that links in the
composition with Jacopo Bellini's
*Agony* in Bellini's London sketch-
book are not decisive, and she stresses
the originality of Mantegna's icono-
graphical detail of the five angels
bearing the implements of Christ's
Passion, instead of the ritual chalice
usually appearing to Christ. She also
suggests a date around 1450, which
is perhaps too early. Also in the
National Gallery is an initial from an
illuminated missal (No. 1417a) which
repeats the motif of the praying
Christ.

Plate 46

THE AGONY IN THE GARDEN.
Detail: a bird.

Plate 47

THE AGONY IN THE GARDEN.
Detail: the sleeping Apostles.

# THE SAN ZENO ALTARPIECE

## (Plates 48–59)

The main part of the polyptych, consisting of the three major panels (220 × 115 each), is in the Church of San Zeno in Verona. It comprises: at the center, an enthroned Virgin and Child surrounded by angels singing and playing instruments; at the left, SS Peter, Paul, John the Evangelist, and Zeno; at the right, SS Benedict, Lawrence, Gregory, and John the Baptist. The predella, also consisting of three panels, is divided between the Louvre (plate 57) and the museum in Tours (plates 56 and 58). These panels are replaced in the Altarpiece by copies set in the original frame. The division of the Altarpiece occurred when the French sacked Verona in 1797. The three major panels, which had also been taken to France, were returned in 1816. The commission for this work was given to Mantegna by the Papal Protonotary, Gregorio Correr, Abbot of San Zeno. The artist began the painting in January 1457 and did not complete it until the end of 1459. The design for the frame is also by Mantegna. Benaglio copied the picture in 1462, with variations (*St Bernardino Triptych*, Verona). Kristeller considers this composition a development of Vivarini's altarpiece of 1446 (see comment on plate 13), but it may be worth while recalling at this point A. Venturi's remarks on Mantegna's gradual approach to Donatello (Mantegna had already transformed the sculptor's bas-reliefs into fully rounded statues in the Ovetari Chapel). Here he reflects the roundness of the altar which Donatello had just completed in Padua. This polyptych, in fact, was painted in Padua and transferred to Venice shortly before the artist's move to Mantua. Restored by Guido Gregorietti in 1947.

### Plate 48
THE SAN ZENO ALTARPIECE. General view.

### Color Plate III
THE AGONY IN THE GARDEN. Detail of plate 45: sleeping Apostles.

### Plate 49
CENTRAL PANEL. General view.

### Plate 50
LEFT-HAND PANEL. General view, with SS Peter, Paul, John the Evangelist, and Zeno.

### Plate 51
RIGHT-HAND PANEL. General view, with SS Benedict, Lawrence, Gregory, and John the Baptist.

### Plate 52
CENTRAL PANEL. Detail: the Angels.

### Plate 53
CENTRAL PANEL. Detail: the Virgin.

### Plate 54
LEFT-HAND PANEL. Detail: architectural elements and festoons in the upper part.

### Plate 55
RIGHT-HAND PANEL. Detail: the medallion with mythological figures on the central pilaster.

### Plate 56
THE AGONY IN THE GARDEN. *Panel, 70 × 92. Tours, Museum*

*Predella of the San Zeno Altarpiece, left wing.* The now divided predella is unanimously considered one of Mantegna's finest achievements. E. Tietze-Conrat, however, believes it to have been painted by the same assistant who she thinks executed the *Adoration of the Shepherds* in the Metropolitan Museum, New York (plate 44).

### Plate 57

THE CRUCIFIXION. *Panel, 67 × 92. Paris, Louvre.* Central section of the San Zeno predella. (See also plate 59.)

### Plate 58

THE RESURRECTION. *Panel, 70 × 92. Tours, Museum.* Predella of the *San Zeno Altarpiece*, right wing. Only E. Tietze-Conrat and Meiss ascribe this part also to Mantegna's workshop. They do concede, however, that the figure of Christ may have been directly inspired by the master. Fiocco has noted an analogy to Andrea del Castagno and some details of Flemish character.

### Plate 59

THE CRUCIFIXION. Detail: rocks and landscape on the left.

### Plate 60

ST GEORGE. *Panel, 66 × 32. Venice, Galleria dell'Accademia.* Moved to its present location in 1856 from the Manfrin Collection. Restored in 1955 by Mauro Pellicioli who removed a number of arbitrary additions from the breastplate and dragon's head. Crowe and Cavalcaselle believe the panel was executed at the time of the Uffizi triptych. Kristeller and Adolfo Venturi think it was painted after the *San Zeno Altarpiece,* and Fiocco, Sandra Moschini (*Catalogo dell' Accademia,* 1955) and Paccagnini consider it later than the Uffizi triptych.

E. Tietze-Conrat dates the painting in the second half of the 1450's, the same time as the *Martyrdom of St James* in the Ovetari Chapel.

### Plate 61

ST SEBASTIAN. *Panel, 68 × 30. Vienna, Kunsthistorisches Museum.* From the collection of Archduke Leopold Wilhelm of Austria. Inscribed in Greek letters: ΤΟ ΕΡΓΟΝ ΤΟΥ ΑΝΔΡΕΟΥ ("the work of Andrea"). In the cloud at the top left is the figure of a horseman, perhaps Theodoric of Verona (Kristeller). Formerly dated about 1450, this painting could be the *operetta* Mantegna executed for the governor of Padua, Antonio Marcello, before the artist left for Mantua in 1459. This dating is now commonly accepted, although Longhi considers that the execution could not have taken place before 1470.

### Plate 62

ST GEORGE. Detail: the Saint's head and landscape.

### Plate 63

ST SEBASTIAN. Detail: the sky and the architecture in the upper left.

### Plate 64

ST SEBASTIAN. Detail: landscape at left.

### Color Plate IV

THE CRUCIFIXION. Detail of plate 57: mourning women.

### Plate 65

ST JEROME IN THE WILDERNESS. *Panel, 48 × 37. São Paulo, Brazil, Art Museum.* Formerly in the collection of Prince Paul of Yugoslavia, for whom it was acquired at Christie's of London in 1936. Part of the rock (top left) disappeared after recent restoration. Published as a work by Mantegna by T. Borenius in 1936, but ascribed to Marco Zoppo by Ragghianti and Fiocco. Berenson accepted it as an autograph Mantegna in 1952.

## Plate 66

THE PRESENTATION IN THE TEMPLE. *Canvas, 67 × 86. Berlin, Staatliches Museen.* Formerly in the Bembo Collection, then in the Gradenigo Collection, Padua, and later in the Solly Collection, London. Acknowledged as an autograph work by Mantegna by Crowe and Cavalcaselle (1871). Morelli (1880) and later A. Venturi considered it an ugly copy of a similar painting in the Querini Stampalia Gallery, Venice. This last is now believed to have been executed by Giovanni Bellini from the magnificent original—the credit for which must undoubtedly go to Mantegna. The canvas was seen by Michiel in the house of Bembo in Padua and is datable about 1454. In 1962 Longhi dated it 1465, approximately the time of the Bellini version. Paccagnini notes Tuscan echoes in this work, and he dates it later than 1466.

## Plate 67

PORTRAIT OF CARDINAL LOD-OVICO MEZZAROTA. *Panel, 44 × 33. Berlin, Staatliches Museen.* From the Solly Collection. The identification of the sitter is based on the portrait's resemblance to a print in *Illustriorum Virorum Elogia* (1630) by Tomasino, and to various medallions. The Cardinal stayed in Mantua during the Council held there by

Pope Pius II between May 27, 1458 and February 8, 1460. The painting is consistent with these dates.

## Plate 68

PORTRAIT OF CARDINAL FRAN-CESCO GONZAGA. *Canvas, 25 × 17.5. Naples, Museo Nazionale di Capodimonte.* In 1697 this portrait was in the Farnese Palace in Rome, and was attributed to Giovanni Bellini's workshop. Frizzoni identified the sitter as Francesco Gonzaga, who was appointed a Bishop in 1462 at the age of sixteen, and portrayed by Mantegna in the *Camera degli Sposi* as he looked in 1474 (see comments on pages 75, 76). This theory is rejected only by Fiocco who believes the work to be a portrait of Lodovico Gonzaga, who was consecrated a Bishop at the age of nine, and is also portrayed in the *Camera degli Sposi*, but shows no more than family likeness to the Naples portrait. It seems more probable that the sitter was Francesco and that the work was painted shortly after 1462. E. Tietze-Conrat, Meiss, Arslan, and Gilbert consider this canvas a repetition of a larger original by Mantegna.

## Plate 69

MADONNA WITH SLEEPING CHILD. *Canvas, 42 × 32. Berlin, Staatliches Museen.* Formerly in the collection of Count della Porta in Vicenza, from where it passed to the Simon Collection in Berlin and thence to its present location. The work was considered by Kristeller to be "closely related to the Saint Eufemia of 1454 in Naples." Arslan agrees with this date, but Paccagnini and Gilbert suggest a date around 1466. Fiocco describes the canvas as an early work and Longhi as "decidedly late."

# THE FLORENCE TRIPTYCH

## (Plates 70–74)

This *Triptych* is in the Uffizi Gallery in Florence. It consists of: in the center, the *Adoration of the Magi* (concave panel, 76 × 76.5); at the left, the *Ascension* (panel, 86 × 43); at the right, the *Circumcision* (panel, 86 × 43). The frame dates from 1827. In 1587 this work was the property of Don Antonio de' Medici, at Valle Muggia, near Pistoia; in 1632 it passed into the Medici Collection in Florence. Fiocco thinks that the *Triptych* could not have originally been in the chapel of Mantua Castle, where Vasari recorded "a small panel, the figures in which are not very large, but are exceedingly beautiful," because in 1657 Scannelli saw some works by Mantegna in the chapel which are known to have been partially executed at Goito in 1464, and must have been fairly numerous. It is also doubtful whether the *Triptych* originally consisted of the three present panels (see comment on plate 76). Represented in the marble lunettes in the upper part of the *Circumcision* are the *Sacrifice of Abraham* and *Moses Giving the Laws*. E. Tietze-Conrat notes a very close relationship between the architecture in this panel and the Cappella del Perdono in Urbino, by L. Laurana, who worked in Mantua around 1465. Recent restorations have brought out more discrepancies between three panels. Several repaints have also been removed from the *Circumcision*. See comment on plate 76 as regards the dating of this panel.

## Plate 70
THE CIRCUMCISION. General view of the panel on the right.

## Plate 71
THE ASCENSION. General view of the panel on the left.

## Plates 72–73
THE ADORATION OF THE MAGI. General view of the central panel. (See also plate 74.)

## Plate 74
THE ADORATION OF THE MAGI. Detail: the kneeling king.

## Plate 75
CHRIST WITH THE ANIMULA OF THE VIRGIN. *Panel, 27.5 × 17.5. Ferrara, Vendeghini Collection.* See comment on plate 76.

## Plate 76
THE DEATH OF THE VIRGIN. *Panel, 54 × 42. Madrid, Prado.* The top section of this panel has been cut off. Longhi discovered the fragment portraying *Christ with the Animula of the Virgin* (plate 75) in the Vendeghini Collection in Ferrara. This enabled him to reconstruct the original appearance of the picture. The measurements were probably the same as those of the wings of the *Florence Triptych*. In fact Longhi believed that this work was originally part of the *Triptych* (1930). Fiocco did not subscribe to this theory, but most other critics did, particularly as the relationship between the *Ascension* and the *Death of the Virgin* is much closer than that between the three panels of the *Triptych*. In 1962 Longhi established the chronological order of the execution, which took several years. He believed the two latter panels were among the first to be painted by

Mantegna during his stay in Mantua; they were followed by the *Adoration of the Magi* and concluded by the *Circumcision,* which the artist perhaps did over and over again and datable before 1473 when Liberale da Verona drew inspiration from it for some of his miniatures. Other scenes from the life of Christ were to decorate the Mantuan chapel: some are quoted in the inventories, others are reproduced in prints of Mantegna's works such as the *Flagellation,* the *Deposition* (with two ladders resting against the Cross), the *Descent into Hell*—a different version from that formerly at Asolo (plate 154) which, from a

letter, we know to have been painted in 1468. Another version of the *Death of the Virgin* was in Ferrara Castle, but the Prado picture comes from the collection of King Charles I of England, for whom it was acquired at Mantua in 1627 with the *Sacra Conversazione* in Boston (plate 155). This last is of doubtful origin, certainly painted later and bearing a false signature, though it, too, seems to have been cut at the top, probably to make it pair with the *Death of the Virgin,* for the two have the same measurements. No one has ever doubted that the *Death of the Virgin* is an autograph work, except for Adolfo Venturi who, revising an earlier opinion, attributed it to Giovanni Bellini (*L'Arte,* 1924) because of its soft colors and the rhythm of the composition. This theory should be rejected. Fiocco thinks that the arrangement of the picture was derived from a similar one in a mosaic in the Mascoli Chapel in Venice (plate 165), which he believes Mantegna to have painted about 1454. Longhi—and this is the most convincing theory—believes that the mosaic was derived from the panel, and that the panel was painted by an imitator of Mantegna. The landscape in the background has been variously identified with lake views in the country around Mantua (plate 77).

### Plate 77

THE DEATH OF THE VIRGIN. Detail: the landscape.

### Plate 78

PORTRAIT OF CARDINAL CARLO DE' MEDICI. *Panel, 40.5 × 29.5. Florence, Uffizi.* The identification of the sitter is due to Emil Schaffer (*Monatshefte fur Kunstwissenschaft,* 1912), and based on the portrait's resemblance to an engraving by

Martino Rota. Before 1912 the sitter was thought to be a member of the Gonzaga family. Kristeller believes the work to be a sixteenth-century copy. E. Tietze-Conrat is also doubtful because of the poor state of preservation. The general opinion, however, is that Mantegna painted this work shortly before the *Camera degli Sposi*, possibly during his stay in Florence in 1466.

## Plate 79

PORTRAIT OF A GENTLEMAN. *Canvas, 24 × 19. Washington, D.C., National Gallery of Art*. From 1906, the property of Balaton Boglar and later of Ludwig Keleman of Budapest; from 1929 in the U.S.A. and from 1950, part of the Samuel Kress Collection. Frankfurter (*Masterpieces of Art*, 1939) identified the sitter with Pannonius—whose portrait Mantegna painted in Padua in 1458 —but this seems impossible, for at the time Pannonius was only about twenty-four years old. The attribution to Mantegna was accepted by Berenson, L. Venturi, W. Suida, and E. Tietze-Conrat, Miess believes it the work of a follower of Mantegna. The date of execution should more or less coincide with the Mantua frescoes.

# LOCATION OF PAINTINGS

ASOLO (formerly)

VALIER COLLECTION
*Christ Descending into Hell* (plate 154; attribution).

BASEL

PRIVATE COLLECTION
*Madonna and Child* (plate 156; attribution).

BERGAMO

ACCADEMIA CARRARA
*Madonna and Child* (plate 138).

BERLIN

STAATLICHES MUSEEN
*The Presentation in the Temple* (plate 66).
*Madonna with Sleeping Child* (plate 69).
*Portrait of Cardinal Lodovico Mezzarota* (plate 67).
*Virgin and Child with Cherubim* (plate 157; attribution).

BOSTON (MASSACHUSSETS)

ISABELLA STEWART GARDNER MUSEUM
*Sacra Conversazione* (plate 155; attribution).

MUSEUM OF FINE ARTS
*Madonna and Child* (plate 158b; attribution).

CINCINNATI (OHIO)

ART MUSEUM
*Tarquinius and the Sibyl* (plate 112).

COPENHAGEN

STATENS MUSEUM FOR KUNST
*Christ Seated on a Sarcophagus and Supported by Two Angels* (plate 141).

CORREGGIO

CONGREGAZIONE DI CARITA
*The Savior* (plate 127).

DRESDEN

GEMÄLDEGALERIE
*Madonna and Child with the Infant St John and Saints* (plate 139).

DUBLIN

NATIONAL GALLERY OF IRELAND
*Judith* (plate 160; attribution).

FERRARA

VENDEGHINI COLLECTION
*Christ with the Animula of the Virgin* (plate 75).

FLORENCE

UFFIZI
*The Florence Triptych* (plates 70–76).

Portrait of Cardinal Carlo de' Medici (plate 78).
The Madonna of the Stonecutters (plates 122–125).

# FRANKFURT-AM-MAIN

STAEDELSCHES KUNSTINSTITUT

St Mark (plate 162; attribution).

# HAMPTON COURT

The Triumphs of Caesar (plates 113–121).

# INVERGARRY (SCOTLAND)

WILLIAM U. GOODBODY COLLECTION

Madonna and Child (plate 158a; attribution).

# LONDON

NATIONAL GALLERY

The Agony in the Garden (plates 45–47).
Virgin and Child with St John the Baptist and Mary Magdalen (plate 134).
The Holy Family with St John (The Infant Christ as Ruler of the World) (plate 140).
The Triumph of Scipio (plates 144, 145).
The Vestal Virgin Tuccia with a Sieve (plate 146a).
Sophonisba (plate 146b).
Samson and Delilah (plate 147).
The Resurrection (plate 178; attribution).
The Three Marys at the Sepulcher (plate 179; attribution).
Noli me Tangere (plate 180; attribution).

# MADRID

PRADO

The Death of the Virgin (plates 76 and 77).

# MANTUA

PALAZZO DUCALE

Mural Decorations in the Camera degli Sposi (plates 80–107).

CHURCH OF SANT' ANDREA

The Holy Family with St John the Baptist and His Parents (plate 159; attribution).

MUSEO DEL PALAZZO DUCALE

Occasio and Paenitentia (plate 161; attribution).

# MILAN

BRERA GALLERY

The St Luke Polyptych (plates 13–21).
Virgin and Child with Cherubim (plate 128).
The Dead Christ (plates 130 and 131).
St Bernardino (plate 164; attribution).

CIVICO MUSEO DEL CASTELLO SFORZESCO

Madonna and Child with Four Saints (plates 135–137).

POLDI PEZZOLI MUSEUM

Virgin and Child (plate 126).
Portrait of a Gentleman (plate 163; attribution).

# MONTREAL

ART ASSOCIATION

Judith (plate 148).
Dido (plate 149).

## NAPLES

MUSEO NAZIONALE DI CAPODIMONTE

*St Euphemia* (plate 32).
*Portrait of Cardinal Francesco Gonzaga* (plate 68).

## NEW YORK

METROPOLITAN MUSEUM OF ART

*Madonna and Child with Cherubim* (plate 31).
*The Adoration of the Shepherds* (plate 44).
*The Holy Family with a Female Saint* (plate 167; attribution).

JACOB M. HEIMANN GALLERY

*The Dead Christ* (plate 168; attribution).

## NORTHAMPTON, CASTLE ASHBY

COLLECTION OF THE MARQUESS OF NORTHAMPTON

*The Adoration of the Magi* (plate 169; attribution).

## PADUA

CHURCH OF THE EREMITANI

*Frescoes in the Ovetari Chape* (plates 1–11, 22–29, 33–43).

MUSEO ANTONIANO

*SS Anthony and Bernardino Holding the Monogram of Christ in a Wreath* (plate 12).

MUSEO CIVICO

*Crouching Soldier* (plate 166; attribution).

## PARIS

LOUVRE

*The Crucifixion* (plate 57).
*St Sebastian* (plates 109–111).
*Madonna della Vittoria* (plates 132, 133).
*Parnassus* (plate 150).
*The Triumph of Virtue* (plate 151).
*Comus, the God of Revelry* (plates 152 and 153).

MUSÉE JACQUEMART-ANDRÉ

*Madonna and Child with SS Jerome and Louis* (plate 170; attribution).
*Virgin and Child with Three Saints* (plate 171; attribution).
*Ecce Homo* (plate 172; attribution).

## SÃO PAULO (BRAZIL)

ART MUSEUM

*St Jerome in the Wilderness* (plate 65).

## TURIN

GALLERIA SABAUDA

*Madonna and Child with the Infant St John and Saints* (plate 129).

## TOURS

MUSEUM

*The Agony in the Garden* (plate 56).
*The Resurrection* (plate 58).

## VENICE

GALLERIE DELL' ACCADEMIA

*St George* (plates 60 and 62).

CA' D'ORO
*St Sebastian* (plate 142).

BASILICA DI SAN MARCO
*The Death of the Virgin* (plate 165; attribution).

## VERONA

BASILICA OF SAN ZENO
MAGGIORE
*The San Zeno Altarpiece* (plates 48–55).

MUSEO DI CASTELVECCHIO
*The Holy Family with a Female Saint* (plate 143).
*Christ Carrying the Cross* (plate 173; attribution).

## VIENNA

KUNSTHISTORISCHES
MUSEUM
*St Sebastian* (plates 61, 63, and 64).
*David with the Head of Goliath* (plate 174; attribution).
*The Sacrifice of Abraham* (plate 175; attribution).

## WASHINGTON, D.C.

NATIONAL GALLERY OF
ART
*The Christ Child Standing in a Niche* (plate 30).
*Portrait of a Gentleman* (plate 79).
*Judith* (plate 108).
*St Jerome* (plate 176; attribution).
*Madonna and Child* (plate 184; attribution).

# REPRODUCTIONS

# ACKNOWLEDGEMENT FOR PLATES

*Alinari, Florence*: plates 9, 18, 19, 52–55, 57, 59, 109–11, 122, 123, 129, 132, 139, 150, 151. *Anderson, Florence*: plates 1–8, 10–13, 16, 20–29, 32–43, 47–51, 60, 62, 68, 70–74, 76–78, 126, 128, 130, 131, 134–8, 142, 147, 159, 164–6. *Berlin, Staatliches Museen*: plates 66, 67, 69, 157. *Boston, Isabella Stewart Gardner Museum*: plate 155. *Boston, Museum of Fine Arts*: plate 158b. *Bulloz, Paris*: plates 56, 58, 152, 153, 170–2. *Bruckmann, Munich*: plate 162. *Cincinnati (Ohio), Art Museum*: plate 112. *Copenhagen, Statens Museum for Kunst*: plate 141. *Dublin, National Gallery of Ireland*: plate 160. *Fiorentini, Venice*: plate 143. *Florence, Uffizi*: plates 124, 125. *Graphic Art Color*: plates 14, 15, 17. *Istituto Grafico Bertieri, Milan*: plates 80–107 and color plate V. *London, National Gallery*: plates 46, 113–21, 140, 144–6. *Manzotti, Correggio*: plate 127. *Milan, Poldi Pezzoli Museum*: plate 163. *Montreal, Museum of Fine Arts*: plates 148, 149. *New York, Metropolitan Museum of Art*: plates 31, 34, 167. *Perotti, Milan*: plate 65. *Scala, Florence*: color plates VII, VIII. *Vienna, Kunsthistorisches Museum*: plates 61, 63, 64, 174, 175. *Washington, D.C., National Gallery of Art*: plates 30, 79, 108, 176.

*Plate 169 is reproduced by courtesy of the Marquess of Northampton. Plates 75, 154, 156, 158a, 161, 168, 173 were obtained from private sources.*

Plate I. HEAD OF A COLOSSUS
formerly in Padua, Church of the Eremitani

Plate 2. SS PETER AND PAUL
formerly in Padua, Church of the Eremitani

Plate 3. ST CHRISTOPHER
formerly in Padua, Church of the Eremitani

Plate 4. THE CALLING OF JAMES AND JOHN
formerly in Padua, Church of the Eremitani

Plate 5. ST JAMES EXPELLING THE DEMONS
formerly in Padua, Church of the Eremitani

Plate 6. ST JAMES BAPTIZING HERMOGENES
formerly in Padua, Church of the Eremitani

Plate 7. ST JAMES BEFORE HEROD AGRIPPA
formerly in Padua, Church of the Eremitani

Plate 8. *Detail of plate 6*

Plate 9. *Detail of plate 6*

Plate 10. *Detail of plate 7*

Plate 11. *Detail of plate 7*

Plate 12. SS ANTHONY AND BERNARDINO HOLDING THE MONOGRAM
OF CHRIST IN A WREATH
Padua, Museo Antoniano

Plate 13. THE ST LUKE POLYPTYCH
Milan, Brera Gallery

Plate 14. *Detail of plate 13*

Plate 15. *Detail of plate 13*

Plate 16. *Detail of plate 13*

THE MARTYRDOM OF ST JAMES
formerly in Padua, Church of the Eremitani
(*detail of plate 23*)

Plate 17. *Detail of plate 13*

Plate 18. *Details of plate 13*

Plate 19. *Details of plate 13*

Plate 20. *Details of plate 13*

Plate 21. *Details of plate 13*

Plate 22. ST JAMES HEALING THE CRIPPLE
formerly in Padua, Church of the Eremitani

Plate 23. THE MARTYRDOM OF ST JAMES
formerly in Padua, Church of the Eremitani

Plate 24. *Detail of plate 22*

Plate 25. *Detail of plate 22*

Plate 26. *Detail of plate 22*

Plate 27. *Detail of plate 22*

Plate 28. *Detail of plate 23*

Plate 29. *Detail of plate 23*

Plate 30. THE CHRIST CHILD STANDING IN A NICHE
Washington, D.C., National Gallery of Art

Plate 31. MADONNA AND CHILD WITH CHERUBIM
New York, Metropolitan Museum of Art

Plate 32. ST EUPHEMIA,
Naples, Museo Nazionale di Capodimonte

THE AGONY IN THE GARDEN
London, National Gallery
(*detail of plate 45*)

Plate 33. THE ASSUMPTION OF THE VIRGIN
Padua, Church of the Eremitani

Plate 34. *Detail of plate 33*

Plate 35. *Detail of plate 33*

Plate 36. THE MARTYRDOM OF ST CHRISTOPHER:
first episode, Padua, Church of the Eremitani

Plate 37. THE MARTYRDOM OF ST CHRISTOPHER:
second episode

Plate 38. *Detail of plate 36*

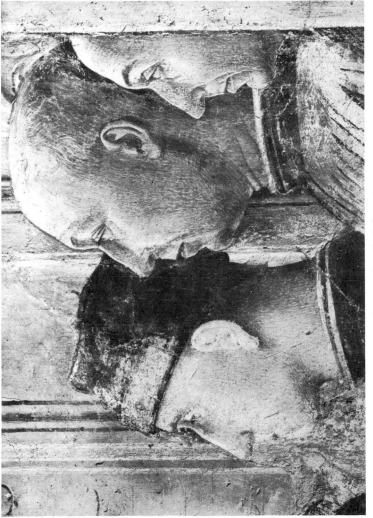

Plate 39. *Detail of plate 36*

Plate 40. *Detail of plate 36*

Plate 41. *Detail of plate 37*

Plate 42. *Detail of plate 37*

Plate 45. THE AGONY IN THE GARDEN
London, National Gallery

Plate 46. *Detail of plate 45*

Plate 47. *Detail of plate 45*

Plate 48. THE SAN ZENO ALTARPIECE
Verona, Church of San Zeno

THE AGONY IN THE GARDEN
London, National Gallery
(*detail of plate 45*)

Plate 49. *Detail of plate 48*

Plate 50. *Detail of plate 48*

Plate 51. *Detail of plate 48*

Plate 52. *Detail of plate 49*

Plate 53. *Detail of plate 19*

Plate 54. *Detail of plate 50*

Plate 55. *Detail of plate 51*

Plate 56. THE AGONY IN THE GARDEN
Tours, Museum

Plate 57. THE CRUCIFIXION
Paris, Louvre

Plate 58. THE RESURRECTION
Tours, Museum

Plate 59. *Detail of plate 57*

Plate 60. ST GEORGE
Venice, Galleria dell'Accademia

Plate 61. THE MARTYRDOM OF ST SEBASTIAN
Vienna, Kunsthistorisches Museum

Plate 62. *Detail of plate 60*

Plate 63. *Detail of plate 61*

Plate 64. *Detail of plate 61*

THE CRUCIFIXION
Paris, Louvre
(*detail of plate 57*)

Plate 65. ST JEROME IN THE WILDERNESS
São Paulo, Art Museum

Plate 66. THE PRESENTATION IN THE TEMPLE
Berlin, Staatliches Museen

Plate 67. PORTRAIT OF CARDINAL LODOVICO MEZZAROTA
Berlin, Staatliches Museen

Plate 68. PORTRAIT OF CARDINAL FRANCESCO GONZAGA
Naples, Museo Nazionale di Capodimonte

Plate 69. MADONNA WITH SLEEPING CHILD
Berlin, Staatliches Museen

Plate 70. THE FLORENCE TRIPTYCH: THE CIRCUMCISION
Florence, Uffizi

Plate 71. THE FLORENCE TRIPTYCH: THE ASCENSION

Plates 72–73. THE FLORENCE T̶

YCH: THE ADORATION OF THE

Plate 74. *Detail of plate 72–73*

Plate 75. CHRIST WITH THE ANIMULA OF THE VIRGIN
Ferrara, Vendeghini Collection

Plate 76. THE DEATH OF THE VIRGIN
Madrid, Prado

Plate 77. *Detail of plate 76*

Plate 78. PORTRAIT OF CARDINAL CARLO DE'MEDICI
Florence, Uffizi

Plate 79. PORTRAIT OF A GENTLEMAN
Washington, D.C., National Gallery of Art